Winning

with the

P&G
99

99 Principles and Practices of Procter & Gamble's Success

Charles L. Decker

POCKET BOOKS
New York   London   Toronto   Sydney   Tokyo   Singapore

This book is not affiliated with, authorized, or endorsed by Proctor & Gamble, Inc.

POCKET BOOKS, a division of Simon & Schuster Inc.
1230 Avenue of the Americas, New York, NY 10020

ISBN: 0-671-01740-3

First Pocket Books trade paperback printing May 1999

10 9 8 7 6 5 4 3 2 1

POCKET and colophon are registered trademarks of Simon & Schuster Inc.

Cover design by Anna Dorfman

Printed in the U.S.A.

to Milt Decker

CONTENTS

2

THE P&G CULTURE   *63*

BELIEFS   *64*

3

MANAGING FOR SUCCESS 105

4

THINK GLOBAL, ACT LOCAL—AND VICE VERSA 133

5

HOW TO SUCCEED AS A P&G BRAND MANAGER 163

6

GOING TO MARKET 187

TRANSFORMING THE PRODUCT INTO A BRAND 188

LESSONS FOR EFFECTIVE
PRINT ADVERTISING

Winning
with the
P&G
99

INTRODUCTION

The Procter & Gamble Company markets over three hundred brands to five billion people around the world. Ninety-eight percent of all homes in America use P&G products. Its products are in the bathroom, the laundry room, the baby's room, the kitchen, the pantry, under the sink, in the medicine cabinet, and in the cosmetics tray.

Although Procter & Gamble's innovations have created or shaped many of the categories that the company competes in—shortening, detergents, disposable diapers—consumers know the company through its brands. P&G's loyal consumers don't buy "shortening," they buy Crisco. They don't buy "laundry detergent," they buy Tide. And to strengthen the bond between its brands and its consumers, P&G spends more than $3 billion a year advertising and promoting its brands—more than any other company in the world.

An extraordinarily creative and innovative company, Procter & Gamble has had an impact on the social landscape and quality of life that goes beyond the many product innovations it has pioneered. P&G is cautious, deliberate,

MAJOR P&G BRANDS

IN THE LAUNDRY ROOM

Tide	Daz*	Ivory Snow
Cheer	Gain	Dreft
Ariel*	Downy	Era
Oxydol	Bounce	Fairy*
Bold	Lenor*	

UNDER THE SINK

Dawn	Cascade	Mr. Clean
Ivory liquid	Spic and Span	Comet
Joy		

IN THE KITCHEN

Bounty	Duncan Hines	Jif
Crisco	Pringles	Sunny Delight
Folgers		

IN THE MEDICINE CABINET

Crest	Scope	Pepto-Bismol
Gleem	Vicks	Didronel
Sure	NyQuil	Fixodent
Secret	Old Spice	Clearasil

IN THE BATHROOM

Pantene	Ivory	Charmin
Head & Shoulders	Zest	Puffs
Pert Plus	Coast	Oil of Olay
Prell	Safeguard	Vidal Sassoon
Camay	Always	

IN THE NURSERY

Pampers	Luvs	Baby Fresh

IN THE COSMETICS TRAY

Cover Girl	Noxzema	Max Factor

*major brands outside the U.S.

and methodical—that's part of the company's culture. But it is also part of P&G's culture to be proactive in looking for not only new and better products but new and better ways to conduct business—leaving its competitors to react to each new initiative. Consider the following three examples.

P&G has been an innovative force in employee relations, having pioneered a shorter workweek over a hundred years ago and the oldest profit-sharing plan in continuous operation in the U.S. The company is still on the forefront of employee relations initiatives—most recently in May 1998 with a grant of stock options to *all* employees (not just management).

P&G had a lot to do with the rapid development of both radio and TV. While other businesses were skeptical about radio in the early 1930s, P&G seized the initiative, developed programming, and dominated the medium. Then, in the early 1950s, the company shifted its advertising budget almost entirely to television, created the daytime "soap opera" and programming (such as *Search for Tomorrow, The Guiding Light, Days of Our Lives, As the World Turns,* and *The Edge of Night*) that, even today, pervades the medium and engages the daily attention of millions of people. P&G continues to view new media as an opportunity to improve its competitive position and is in the vanguard of advertisers aggressively expanding their presence in cable and on the Internet.

P&G also played an important role in the evolution of the ubiquitous and highly efficient supermarket retail distribution system. In 1920, ninety-five percent of the grocery trade was controlled by wholesalers who supplied independent retail grocery stores. But wholesaler buying patterns were erratic, often coming in great surges. That was highly inefficient for P&G and all the other grocery product manufacturers because it required major surges in production followed by plant slowdowns or shutdowns and employee layoffs. P&G dared to challenge the power of the wholesalers by increasing its sales force fourfold and selling direct to the retailer. P&G prevailed despite bitter resistance from both the wholesalers and the retailers themselves, and soon other grocery manufacturers also began to sell direct. The power of the wholesalers was broken, and the stage was set for the evolution of the supermarket retail distribution system. P&G continues to impact the grocery retail distribution system with its initiatives, as will be discussed later in this book.

Although most consumers know Procter & Gamble only through its brands, the company itself is well known and widely admired in the business community:

- For eight consecutive years, P&G has ranked among the top ten of the most-admired corporations in the U.S. in *Fortune* magazine's annual survey.
- It is a $35 billion global empire that has consistently outperformed the Dow Jones average by a wide margin. The company has increased dividends to shareholders for forty-two years in a row. In the *Fortune* survey, it was regarded as one of the top-rated companies for "value as a long-term investment."
- P&G is regarded as one of the best-managed companies in the world. Harvard Business School teaches P&G's heralded brand management system, which the company pioneered in 1931. That system has been emulated by countless companies.
- P&G gets high marks in the *Fortune* survey for its "ability to attract, develop, and keep talented people."

Every year, P&G hires over a thousand graduates from the world's best colleges and graduate schools: engineers, chemists, physicists, biologists, doctors, dentists, business school graduates, and so on. In the U.S. in brand management alone, P&G hires about one hundred recruits to meet the high level of attrition in the very demanding brand-management environment. Brand management represents only about five percent of management-level employees. However, the brand management gauntlet feeds ninety percent of the general management positions in the company and is the route to the very top of the organization. Only a few make it. Most people in brand management leave on their own initiative, lured by other opportunities or to escape a culture that is not to their liking. Some find career track opportunities more suitable to them within P&G. Others are encouraged to continue their careers elsewhere— with the grounding in marketing and management that will serve them for the rest of their lives.

The brand management system works for Procter & Gamble because it is supported by the fundamental belief that spawned the system in the first place: consumers don't buy just products, they buy brands. As the brand is central to the company's success, the brand manager is central to the way the company is organized. But brand managers are not given free rein to do whatever they want with their brands. They are expected to manage their brands with the same analytical approach, thoroughness, and professionalism that is expected from everyone in the company.

Most companies, especially packaged-goods companies, regard P&G training as better than an MBA degree. Recruiting P&G marketers is a sizable cottage industry within the business community. For other packaged-goods companies and advertising agencies, P&G is a primary source of junior and midlevel executives, who, not infrequently, rise to the top of those organizations (for example, former CEOs Jim Ferguson, at General Foods; Jim Burke, at Johnson & Johnson; Bill Phillips, at Ogilvy & Mather; Bill Dunlap, at Campbell-Mithun). And some of the major non–packaged-goods corporations that today dominate their industry sectors have been led by ex-P&Gers. John Smale, former chairman and CEO of P&G, took over as chairman of General Motors in the fall of 1992; Bob Herbold made it to the eleventh-floor executive suite at P&G before he was tapped as COO of Microsoft; John Hanley moved to Monsanto as CEO; Steve Case founded America Online.

Some of the principles, practices, and beliefs that make P&G what it is today can be traced back to the beliefs and ethics of the company's founders, William Procter and James Gamble. These principles, practices, and beliefs evolved into a corporate culture of operating and thinking that has stood the test of time.

The policy of promoting from within, for example, may historically have had something to do with P&G's head-quarter location in Cincinnati—a relatively isolated place compared to New York City, the location of such competitors as Colgate-Palmolive and Lever Brothers, both of whom have readily recruited from each other and from the many other consumer-products companies in the area. But, more important, P&G's policy of promoting from within evolved out of the company's concern for its people, its sense of self-reliance, and the value it places on developing a body of knowledge and learning from its past experiences.

This book grew out of a deep respect that I developed for Procter & Gamble during the five years that I was there in brand management. And during the thirty years or so since I left, as I worked with over twenty other consumer products clients, I came to appreciate how different P&G is in its beliefs and culture and ways of doing things. Many of P&G's principles can be applied or adapted to other companies, and the principles or practices that are not appropriate for certain companies are still instructive, providing insights for those seeking alternative approaches.

Winning with the P&G 99 will present P&G's marketing, business-management, and career-development principles and practices in a way that will enable readers to understand how these have been so successful for P&G and the implications they might have for other companies or other individuals. Their application is not limited to packaged-goods companies and their products. There are implications for just about any business and even for academic, government, and nonprofit organizations. Anyone with a customer, a subordinate, or a boss can gain new insights from these lessons.

My interest in Procter & Gamble, business principles and practices, and consumer marketing does not end with the publication of this book. If you have any comments or suggestions about anything in this book—or even relevant anecdotes—I would be eager to hear from you.

—CHARLIE DECKER
Pelham, New York
CharlieDec@AOL.com

CHAPTER

1

GUIDING PRINCIPLES

There are four guiding principles that are the bedrock of everything that Procter & Gamble does:

The Consumer Is Queen
Build Superior Products
Create Unique Brands
Maintain a Long-term View

They are the foundation for the company's marketing methodologies, rituals, culture, style, and manner of doing business.

THE CONSUMER IS QUEEN

It should surprise no one that P&G is attentive to the consumer. By now the importance of being responsive to the consumer or customer has been well documented in business books and the trade press. What is significant in the case of P&G is not so much the principle itself but the intensity of P&G's efforts to understand the consumer and the rigor with which it applies this overarching principle to everything the company does. It's not only a methodology, it's an attitude.

LESSON 1

Trust the consumer.

The consumer is discerning and discriminating. She carefully weighs the relative merits of available products against their relative costs. The manufacturer who offers real value will be rewarded.

> We will provide products of superior quality and value that improve the lives of the world's consumers. As a result, consumers will reward us with leadership sales and profit growth. . . .
>
> **—from P&G's official Statement of Purpose**

This statement sounds like a boilerplate pronouncement that could come from any number of companies. But in Procter & Gamble's case, it's not just lip service to a theme that sounds nice. P&G works hard to understand and serve consumer needs and desires. It believes that the consumer, who for P&G is usually a female, is the final arbiter of who wins and who loses in the marketplace. P&G trusts the consumer because it has bet the company's future on the consumer being able to recognize the quality and value of P&G brands.

A P&G assistant brand manager once recommended enlarging the opening of the Crest toothpaste tube so that the consumer would use up the toothpaste at a faster rate. Bad idea. It was a cheat. Besides, the consumer is not a fool; she will adjust. The consumer will decide for herself exactly how much product to use. P&G learned that lesson years ago when it tried to market Tide Sheets, premeasured portions of Tide detergent with bleach and fabric softener, and Salvo, the "hockey puck" detergent, in tablet form. Both of these innovations failed because the consumer wants the flexibility to use more or less detergent depending on the size of the washload, what types of fabrics are being washed, and how dirty the clothes are.

That kind of understanding and respect for the consumer encourages P&G to pioneer such products as concentrated detergent products. P&G surprised everyone when it launched "ultra 2" products across its line of detergent brands. This was a risky move. Consumers might have misunderstood the concentrated-formula concept; they might have resisted paying the same amount of money for less product. Or if they did purchase the "ultra 2" product, they might have overused the product, perceived it to be of less value, and stopped buying it. Neither was a problem. Consumers figured it out and adjusted. Ultimately, the consumer benefited from lower prices that resulted from lower packaging and shipping costs, the retail trade benefited from a higher rate of product turnover in less shelf space, and P&G benefited from increased share of market.

P&G even adds value for the consumer in ways that might be expected to actually *reduce* the amount of product the consumer uses. For example, P&G offers a pick-a-size version of Bounty towels with perforations that enable the consumer to use only half a towel for the small jobs. And it offers a rinse-and-reuse version of Bounty that certainly slows the use-up rate but improves the value for the consumer. The company figures consumers will recognize the value and reward these brands with their purchase decision.

Never try to fool the consumer.

You can't get away with trying to market inferior products. Even minor product-performance advantages or disadvantages are important and will be rewarded or punished by the consumer.

Procter & Gamble believes that a real performance advantage, even a small one, is the difference between winning and being an also-ran. Marketing is not a substitute for product performance. Rather, the product advantage gives marketing its leverage. The packaging copy, advertising, and promotional materials all work together to tell the consumer what the brand is all about and the benefits she should be looking for. Small differences in the performance of frequently used products become increasingly noticeable as the consumer experiments with different brands over time. The brand that delivers on its performance promise should come out on top.

The product "blind test"—research that pits two unidentified products against each other in consumers' homes—is a crucial piece of research for every P&G brand. If a brand doesn't have a blind-test win versus the key competition, it doesn't go to market. If, on the other hand, a competitive brand improves its product and wins in a blind test, it's a very big problem for the brand manager and product development department. The brand is considered seriously troubled until it corrects the deficiency.

This kind of respect for the consumer's ability to recognize real product performance is not universal, and it doesn't even exist in some other consumer-products companies. To illustrate, when P&G's Brigade toilet bowl cleaner was successfully launched in a test market, a competing company copied the cosmetics of the product in every respect it could—same color, same scent, same package configuration, and so on. They even printed some arbitrary numbers on the package, replicating some package control numbers on the Brigade package. The numbers didn't mean anything, but the consumer didn't know that. But this company couldn't replicate the formulation of the product itself, and the product did not work. It never even made it out of its test market. The point is, it's unimaginable to think of that happening in the P&G culture. It reflected blatant disrespect for the consumer—to think that she would pay a premium price for a product and not recognize that it was a fake.

LESSON **3** ————————————————————

Value is what the consumer says it is.

The consumer's sensitivity to value has been validated by countless wins—and a few losses—in the marketplace.

Value is not a matter of price alone. If it were, the so-called price brands (generic brands, private label, or "own label" brands of supermarket chains), which sell in the U.S. at anywhere from a ten to twenty percent discount, would have a higher share of the market than national brands marketed by P&G and its competitors. This is not the case. Price brands in grocery stores typically have less than a twenty-five percent share of the market. In Britain "own-label" brands of the major supermarket chains are perceived as being of better quality and control about thirty-five percent of the market. Still, most consumers choose among the higher-priced national brands. For most consumers, the performance superiority of the national brands more than offsets the lower price of the price brands.

$$\text{Value} = \frac{\text{Perceived Benefit}}{\text{Price}}$$

The Perceived Benefit part of the value equation can offset even wide disparities in price. In China, for example, P&G shampoo brands are three times more expensive than local brands. Yet P&G sells half the shampoo in China. The perceived quality of the P&G brands is worth the premium price to the Chinese consumer.

But Price sometimes dominates the value equation. If the Price is too high relative to the Perceived Benefit, the consumer simply won't pay it. If it is not an acceptable value, she'll just do without. That was an important lesson that was learned from P&G's initial efforts to market a disposable diaper.

The invention of Pampers.

The value equation was critical to the success of Pampers disposable diapers. P&G did not invent the disposable diaper. When P&G's first Pampers product was developed, there were several brands of disposable products available to the consumer, and over eighty percent of homes with infants had them on hand. However, disposable diapers were used in only about 0.2 percent of the billions of diaper changes in the U.S. Consumers felt that the quality of the available disposable diaper products was not as good as that of cloth and, more important, the price of about 8.6 cents each made them too expensive for regular use. So they were used just for emergencies, such as when the family was traveling. Thus, the market for disposable diapers was practically nonexistent.

But the Pampers product P&G had developed was far superior to other disposable diapers, and it could be produced and sold at ten cents per diaper, a price that was only slightly higher than the price of inferior competitive brands. So the first Pampers test market was opened in Peoria, Illinois. P&G thought that a sales volume objective based on 2.5 percent of total diaper changes would be reasonable, especially since more than thirty percent of mothers in consumer tests preferred the product over cloth diapers. The test market flopped. Volume was equivalent to only about 0.8 percent of diaper changes. The price of ten cents per diaper was just too much to pay on a regular basis no matter how good the product was.

P&G had to bring the cost down further, and the only

way to do that was to set a sales volume objective that was even higher than the original goal based on 2.5 percent of total diaper changes. If a higher volume level could be achieved, it would enable improved production efficiencies, advertising economies of scale, and set the stage for a cooperative development effort with suppliers to squeeze the cost of goods. Higher volume would also result in a higher rate of shelf turnover, which would enable P&G to persuade supermarkets to distribute the product. Until then, disposable diapers were sold through drugstores, which were not particularly concerned about the low rate of shelf turnover because with a high profit markup they still made money. Supermarkets operated on lower profit margins but required higher shelf turnover.

After three more test markets, the company finally struck a bargain with the consumer. If P&G would price the diapers at six cents each, she would use them on a regular basis. In the final test market, consumption was nearly ten times higher than the original test-market goal based on 2.5 percent of diaper changes. Today nearly ninety-eight percent of all diaper changes are made with disposable diapers, and P&G has more than a third of the market.

Selling detergents in Russia.

In a more recent experience with the value perceptions of consumers, P&G launched its laundry detergent business in Russia in 1992 with the introduction of Ariel—the company's leading detergent brand in Europe. Research showed that Russian homemakers loved the product. So it was introduced into the marketplace. Three months after the launch, eighty-five percent of consumers were aware of it. But only five percent had bought it. The other ninety-five percent simply couldn't afford it. Therefore, P&G introduced Tix detergent, a good formula, but less expensive to produce and priced lower. This was still not low enough. Finally, they introduced a third brand in "polybags," rather than boxes, and found a way to produce it locally at a huge cost savings. They used the name Tide. Although the Russian and American products are different, Tide is now the number one selling detergent brand in both countries.

LESSON 4 ────────────────────────────

Find out what she wants and how she wants it.

Procter & Gamble is generally credited with being the first major consumer-products company to build its success on, first, thoroughly understanding the consumer's needs through a rigorous, systematic consumer research program and then developing the right products and marketing programs to meet those needs.

Procter & Gamble people have an insatiable appetite for understanding and getting feedback from the consumer. As one former P&G researcher put it, "Unlike a lot of other companies, Procter really does use the research that they do. They like to listen to their consumers." Another sixteen-year veteran of the P&G market research department said, "They really *believe* in [research]. They don't just do it as a routine thing; they do it with genuine interest in finding out. . . . They're really curious. They believe in the results; then they act on [that belief]."

From the product idea to the marketing of a brand, P&G is eagerly attentive to the consumer at every step of the way.

"Church panels" are frequently used by the product development group at an early stage. The churchwomen visit "stations" that P&G sets up in the church basement to test a variety of projects in development—alternative colors for facial tissues, variations of peanut butter, alternative safety packages for a prescription drug, and so forth. The results from these panels are not conclusive or projectable, but they provide a reality check for the product development team, who would otherwise make decisions based on judgment uninformed by any consumer input.

As products become more refined, home performance tests are used by product development to evaluate a range of product-related issues in actual home-use conditions. Once product development is satisfied, the brand group gets involved and takes the lead. At that stage, the focus of the research becomes more marketing oriented, and a blind test would be conducted before the product is taken to the market.

No important decisions are made unless they can be supported by research.

LESSON **5** ———————————————————

Find out what she doesn't know she wants.

The consumer will tell you what she **thinks** *she wants or which product she prefers if presented with alternatives. But the consumer cannot be expected to envision a product for which there is no frame of reference or a solution to a problem she doesn't know she* **has.**

In the 1800s static in clothing, stains that wouldn't come out, and cavities in children's teeth were facts of life. Few people thought of them as problems. No one had yet envisioned products such as Bounce, Tide, and Crest.

P&G looks beyond what consumers say they want. P&G digs into consumers' attitudes and behaviors for any hints that might reveal a "problem" that the consumer doesn't know she has or an opportunity to make her life easier or more pleasant.

Pioneering *in situ* research.

For example, P&G was a pioneer of *in situ* research in which researchers go into consumers' homes to observe them directly as they go about their daily lives—from the bathroom to the kitchen to the laundry room and back. A former vice president and general manager at P&G (responsible for a category of products in the laundry and cleaning products division) recalled a study in the 1970s in which consumers were observed opening detergent packages with screwdrivers, razors, or whatever was handy. No problem.

That's the way it had always been. The result was P&G's patented invention of the "easy-open box," which incorporated a plastic insert in the cardboard. That design is in common use today.

Another example was the invention of a "dripless spout" for liquid detergent bottles—a simple redesign of the spout that funnels any drips right back into the bottle. There was no perceived need for this spout. The "need" was discovered by an *in situ* researcher who observed that some of the liquid laundry detergent, when poured, would run down the front of the bottle. The women she observed did not perceive that to be a problem—they simply wiped the drip with the nearest piece of dirty laundry before tossing it into the washing machine. The consumer response to the dripless-spout solution for this nonproblem resulted in millions of dollars in increased sales.

Conducting research in Eastern Europe.

In situ research has been particularly valuable when entering new and unfamiliar markets. P&G's entry into Eastern Europe is a good example of this at work.

After the Berlin Wall came down in the fall of 1989, P&G didn't just tiptoe in, introducing one product category in one country at a time—as it had in Western Europe over the previous several decades. The race was on. It blitzed into several countries with five to seven categories almost simultaneously. But not without first blitzing those countries with a massive research program.

P&G conducted fifty thousand consumer interviews. One of the first things their researchers did was basic *in situ* research to learn how household products fit into Eastern European lives. The researchers were surprised at how small living quarters are. The average apartment or home houses four people in living space of about fifty square feet per person, compared to an average of about 660 square feet per person in the U.S. The living room in some homes is also the dining room, and the coffee table becomes the dining room table. At night, they move the table aside to pull out the bed, because the living room is also a bedroom.

The laundry is generally done in the adjacent bathroom. The only detergent available was a state-made product that required hours of presoaking and filled the entire apartment with a rancid chemical odor that hung around even after the wash was finished. P&G had known that there was a need for a better *cleaning* product, but consumers didn't think to tell the researchers about the offensive *odor*. And the researchers had no reason to ask. Only by living with the laundry process inside the home did they gain the insight that fragrance would be nearly as important as cleaning power to these consumers. P&G ultimately launched three detergent brands at different price points and became the leading detergent manufacturer in the Eastern European market.

LESSON **6** ————————————————

Listen carefully. It's easy to misunderstand the consumer.

Methodology pitfalls can result in flawed research.

P&G is meticulous and precise in its research methodologies. It works hard to avoid bias and use information objectively and critically.

This rigorous, systematic approach to consumer research came about more by happenstance than by calculated design—thanks to the curiosity and persistence of Dr. Paul Smelser.

"Doc Smelser," as he is referred to by former P&G researchers, was hired in 1923 to set up a first-of-its-kind economic research department to help anticipate fluctuations in the commodities market. But Doc Smelser's curiosity spilled over into consumer marketing. He asked questions that Cooper Procter (the third-generation president) and the top officers of the company couldn't answer—relevant questions about how and why consumers used P&G products, what they liked about them, and what they might like better about them. So top management gave him free rein to find the answers. He did and, in the process, launched a pioneering consumer-research operation that evolved into what is arguably the premier research organization of the packaged-goods business today.

Ask the right questions.

One of the things that Doc Smelser discovered was that consumers would often misinterpret questions that seemed to him to be straightforward. And, even if they did understand the question, consumers' answers could be ambiguous. There is an art to asking the right questions and helping the consumer to clarify her answers. The methodologies he developed are used by P&G researchers today.

For example, P&G interviewers don't ask a consumer why she *doesn't* use Tide detergent. She can't relate to that. Or whether she would use Tide if . . . That's hypothetical, and her answer might be influenced by what she thinks the interviewer might want to hear. She *can* relate to what she actually does use and why. "I use All detergent because it's low sudsing and . . ." This gives the interviewer the opportunity to follow up with questions that truly reflect the consumer's thinking. "Tell me more about low sudsing."

P&G interviewers are also trained to identify ambiguity in consumers' answers and to probe until the true meaning is clear. If a consumer says she uses a certain brand of shampoo because it does the best job of getting her hair clean, what does she mean by "clean"? Does "clean" mean the way it feels or the way it looks? Does "clean" mean free of dirt or nongreasy or free of dandruff or a less itchy scalp? Is "clean" hair squeaky, slippery, lively, bouncy, fluffy, shiny, easy-to-comb, or manageable?

All consumers are not alike; understand the differences and define your research target.

If you are selling Jif peanut butter, it's a good idea to talk to people who eat peanut butter or who buy it for their kids. If you're selling Head & Shoulders shampoo, you'll probably want to talk with people who get dandruff. If you are selling Clearasil acne medication, you'll want to talk with kids who get pimples. This is pretty obvious.

But, the answers you get from these groups of consumers might mask some important differences among segments within the groups. So if you're selling Clearasil, you need to know if the different perspectives of girls versus boys or of preteens versus teens would result in different responses to the research. Also, should you narrow your research target to frequent users of acne medication or to infrequent users or to nonusers who might be converted? Or to consumers loyal to your brand or to users who switch back and forth between brands or to users loyal to competitive brands? The answer depends on your objectives.

Be careful about opinions that get tangled up in perceptions.

What if you developed a new detergent that is just as gentle on delicate fabrics as other brands in the mild-detergent category but cleans better? If you blind-test it among users of mild detergent brands, it might win. But if you took it into the marketplace and told users of mild detergent brands that it cleaned better than their current brand, they might be concerned about whether it would damage their clothes. The perception of cleaning power can be incompatible with that of mildness. This perception would have to be addressed if the product were to succeed in the marketplace.

P&G had a similar difficulty in interpreting product testing for its Citrus Hill orange juice brand. The taste of Citrus Hill was preferred by a whopping 60–40 margin in blind tests. However, taste is very subjective and, in the orange juice category, is linked to consumer perceptions of freshness. Tropicana orange juice was perceived as being fresher. Even the variation of Tropicana juice from thick to watery supported the brand's freshness positioning; it was perceived to be a result of the natural variation from one batch of fresh oranges to another. (P&G had developed processing improvements to eliminate that kind of variability.) So when consumers knew they were drinking Tropicana, a fresher, "real" orange juice product, it was perceived as being better tasting. P&G concluded that orange juice is a commodity business that can't be readily enhanced by product technology, and it sold its Citrus Hill brand.

No information is better than bad information.

The quality and reliability of information gets a lot of attention at P&G. Data are continuously checked and validated. Information that is questionable is carefully identified as such or ignored.

This belief also traces back to Doc Smelser. He believed that research could be misleading that *no research* was better than the *wrong research*. When his department was asked to determine the most appealing fragrance for Camay soap, his first research procedure was to ask women to smell the perfumes directly. He learned later that the smell of a perfume is different when it is diluted to become part of a soap, and its strength can change as the soap is used and melts down. The initial research was trashed. From then on, soaps, toothpastes, and everything else would be tested *in use* before any final decisions were made.

The research disciplines that prevent the misuse of data remain at the heart of P&G's research methodologies today. For example, when quantitative research results are reported, the statistical significance of the data is also reported. Numbers that might be a result of statistical variation rather than a reflection of real differences in the marketplace are flagged or replaced by asterisks.

Preserve the integrity of the data.

Beyond his basic curiosity, Doc Smelser was something of a purist and believed that, to maintain objectivity, it was important to separate the facts from any implications and actions they might suggest. He strongly believed his research reports should contain facts, not editorial matter, and that the person who requested the study should be able to come to his own conclusions as to what action was called for.

That belief is carried forward today. When the market research department reports the findings of a completed research project to the brand group, it is careful not to analyze the data the researchers have gathered. As Ellen Lady, a former research brand supervisor, put it, "The mission was to report the data without *saying* anything with the data." The reason? It is felt that, once you begin to look for conclusions that come out of the data, you risk becoming a proponent for your interpretation, introducing a bias that could distort an objective presentation of the data. The brand group, not the research department, analyzes the information.

But the role of the market research department does not end with the data report. The brand group analysis of the data will include a statement, such as the following, at the very beginning of the memo: "MRD [Jane Doe] agrees that this summary is technically correct and consistent with the findings." And in the right-hand margin next to that sentence will be Jane's scribbled initials. The brand group is required to get the research brand supervisor to sign off on the analysis in order to assure that the data are not being misinterpreted. This is not taken lightly by the research brand supervisor. The reports and analyses that the brand supervisor has signed off on are carefully reviewed by the supervisor's boss. So the meetings between the brand group and brand supervisor are often animated, but the net result is a well-forged analysis grounded in solid, well-understood data.

What happens when the brand supervisor won't sign off? An impasse seldom happens, but, in the words of former P&G chairman Brad Butler, "When a question exists and the answer isn't readily apparent, our management structure ensures that at least two points of view will emerge. The resolution of such differences . . . dramatically increases the probability that the final decision will be made on the basis of wisdom and knowledge rather than on the basis of individual opinion."

Use qualitative research carefully.

P&G is careful in its use of qualitative research, such as focus groups. It uses a lot of focus groups to gain insights— such as to explore whether using a fabric softener has any perceived connection with being a good mom or what kinds of reactions consumers might have to a new way of demonstrating Bounty paper towels' absorbency. But P&G doesn't make broad generalizations and major decisions based on three or four focus groups. The stated purposes for focus groups, as submitted in requests for them by product development or the brand groups, are "to develop hypotheses for further exploration" or "to *help* design" a quantitative study or "to get *preliminary* consumer reactions" to product concepts. The request procedure assures that the research does not overreach its capability.

The research training program.

The importance that P&G places on the methodologies to collect meaningful and reliable data is underscored by a description of its research training program. Rick Snyder's experience is typical. Snyder had earned his MBA at Ohio State University and was hired to be a research brand supervisor to consult with brand managers on their research needs, develop questionnaires, supervise fieldwork, and summarize the results. But he went through more than a year of training before he was deemed qualified to do the job he was hired for.

For his first month with the company, he spent eight hours a day, five days a week, conducting telephone interviews with real consumers and collecting data. But the data would never be used. The interviews were purely for his training. A trainer was by his side, debriefing him after every call. He learned how consumers respond to questions, how consumers talk, and how questions can be misinterpreted. He learned how to ask brand-usage questions, attribute-rating questions, and open-ended questions; how to identify incomplete or ambiguous responses; and how to probe for more complete, precise answers.

After the first month, he spent a year as a field interviewer, conducting telephone or face-to-face interviews for a variety of P&G research projects. As a field interviewer, he expanded his understanding of how consumers relate to the questions that are asked. But more than that, he learned how to interact with consumers and make the research interview feel like a conversation. He even learned to memorize the structure of the interview so that he did not need to use a questionnaire. Snyder said, "I learned more about marketing research in that year of interviewing than I have in the subsequent twenty years."

LESSON 7

Keep listening after the sale is made.

Most companies have a customer relations department of some kind. Some narrowly think of customer relations as a function that deals with or deflects complaints. P&G thinks of customer relations as an opportunity. P&G actively solicits and responds to feedback from anyone who uses its brands—and, in the process, strengthens the relationship with the consumer.

P&G has responded to consumer letters for as long as can be remembered. Letters, or verbatim excerpts of letters and E-mails, and summaries of incoming calls are routinely circulated to brand managers, product development, production, and top management.

In the 1970s, the company began to follow up some of the correspondence with phone calls to get more input and to respond more fully. Then the Duncan Hines brand group decided to solicit consumer reactions to Duncan Hines brownie mix with an 800 number on the package. By 1981 there was an 800 number on *every* P&G package.

The company now gets over three million phone calls a year. The customer relations people who answer the phones receive ongoing training about P&G brands and how to explain how to use products, and how to respond to complaints. They also "work" those calls to catch problems early on or to spot emerging trends.

Customer relations as an early warning system.

For example, in an upgrade of the Pampers and Luvs diapers, the design of the fastening tape had to be modified. The redesign resulted in an infrequent manufacturing defect that was not picked up in development or in routine plant inspections. Parents were irate when the fabric of the diaper tore when they tried to open the fastening tape. As soon as the first few calls came in, manufacturing was notified, and the problem was quickly corrected. The consumers who had called in were called back, thanked for having called, reassured that the problem had been fixed, and sent a sample of the revised product as a gesture of goodwill.

Customer relations as a research tool.

In another example, the number one consumer inquiry regarding Oil of Olay lotion was whether it came in an unscented version. Not surprisingly, the brand group took the cue and developed an unscented version. What is significant—and reveals the quality of the contact that the telephone operators have with the consumer—is that the brand group conducted focus groups among the telephone operators who handle the Oil of Olay calls to help brainstorm for key benefits. Additional focus groups were conducted with the telephone operators to review the words the brand group was considering using on the package. When the unscented product was brought to market, all the consumers who had called initially were called back, thanked, told that the product was available, and sent a free sample or high value coupon.

Building relationships with the consumer.

Charlotte Otto, senior vice president of public affairs, sums it up this way: "We may market our brands to nearly five billion consumers, but our brands build relationships with those consumers one by one. And that's why consumer relations is such a powerful source of competitive advantage. Because they deal with consumers the same way. One by one."

BUILD SUPERIOR PRODUCTS

As a corollary to P&G's respect for the consumer, P&G's mission is to develop products that provide real value to the consumer.

LESSON **8** —————————————————————

Invest in innovation.

Better products don't just happen. The company that is committed to being a leader in the science and technology of the categories in which it competes will be the company that consistently develops the best products.

> People think of P&G as a marketing company, but we are first and foremost a research-and-development company. R&D is the lifeblood of our business.
>
> **—John Pepper, P&G CEO**

P&G holds more than 2,500 active patents, protecting 250 proprietary technologies. It employs 7,000 scientists working in its seventeen research centers around the world. Among them there are 1,250 PhD scientists, which is more than are in the combined science departments of Harvard, MIT, Stanford, Tokyo University, and London's Imperial College.

The milestones of the company's success are marked by major product innovations resulting from technology breakthroughs, inventions, and reapplication of technologies to other product categories:

Ivory (1879)	—the first all-purpose soap that didn't give the baby a rash
Floating Ivory (also 1879)	—the first floating bar soap
Crisco (1911)	—the first all-vegetable shortening
Tide (1946)	—the first heavy-duty synthetic laundry detergent

Crest (1955)	—the first fluoride toothpaste
Comet (1956)	—the first scouring cleanser with effective bleaching
Pampers (1956)	—the first effective, economically priced disposable diaper
Head & Shoulders (1961)	—the first effective dandruff-control shampoo
Bounce (1972)	—the first dryer-added fabric softener
Didronel (1978)	—the first prescription drug that reversed bone loss for those susceptible to osteoporosis
Liquid Tide, Ariel, and Vizir (1984)	—the first liquid laundry detergents that cleaned as well as powders
Tartar Control Crest (1985)	—the first toothpaste with an effective tartar control formula

Major new technologies often take many years to develop and even more years to perfect. The Pampers story described in Lesson #3 began in 1954. It took more than ten years just to figure out how to make the product and produce it for national distribution. Along the way came some key inventions, such as the porous sheet between the baby and the absorbent material that allowed fluid to pass through to the absorbent material but prevented most of it from coming back. But that was only the beginning. In 1967 researchers developed a "woven" wet fiber molding process that produced a three-dimensional paper structure using less wood fiber but resulting in softer, stronger, more absorbent paper. They continued to perfect the process and, in 1985, patented paper-making processes that non-P&G scientists had earlier deemed impossible to achieve.

It took fifteen years from the time that stannous fluoride

was identified as a potential anticavity fighter to the introduction of Crest toothpaste in 1955.

Pringles "newfangled potato chips" was a dismal failure for a quarter of a century. But P&G didn't give up. It had developed a technology that made uniform, elliptical chips from dehydrated potatoes that could be stacked in a "tennis-ball container" to keep them from breaking or becoming stale—a problem for conventional bagged potato chips. But the consumer loved the taste of real potato chips. It took P&G years to figure out how to get the taste right. Then a few more years to find the marketing handle. Now the brand is not only considered a big success in the U.S., Pringles is P&G's number one export brand.

Pantene was a very small shampoo brand that came along with P&G's Richardson-Vicks acquisition in 1985. It was a good product with the mystique of a high-priced department store brand. P&G made some pricing and distribution changes to increase its sales volume, but it was still a minor brand in the category. But when P&G converted it into a shampoo-and-conditioner product with their patented "2-in-1" technology, the brand took off and is now a global billion-dollar brand.

Olestra is a fat substitute that tastes like a fat and fries like a fat, but does not digest like a fat. The body just enjoys it for a while then passes it on through. Although olestra has caused some unpleasant digestive problems along the way, P&G claims to have fixed these problems and now has the approval of the Food and Drug Administration. Olestra is a breakthrough technology that CEO John Pepper thinks is going to be "viewed in history as one of the real benchmark innovations in this company." The technology began its evolutionary journey in the P&G labs over thirty years ago. P&G went through several fits and starts in regard to what olestra was and what it would be used for. P&G also went through many back-and-forths with the FDA. But patience and persistence reigned, along with a few hundred million dollars, and Olean, P&G's trademark name for its fat substitute, is the result. It is a potential multibillion-dollar business.

The point here is to look ahead. P&G spends over $1.3 billion a year on research and development, looking for next year's product improvements as well as major innovations that could be decades away from marketplace reality. Over the years, P&G spending has consistently exceeded its rivals' spending in both dollars and as a percentage of sales.

LESSON **9** ————————————————

Err on the side of technology.

Products based on new technologies don't always succeed at first. Have some tolerance for mistakes; rework the products or try to address consumer reservations.

P&G has a great deal of patience with products built on new or superior technologies. Some would call it technology myopia. Others would call it a part of the company's investment in technology. That patience and persistence has paid off for major brands such as Pampers, Crest, Pringles, and Pantene.

It is understandable that P&G would also have a few products that didn't make it. No one at P&G wants to kill a new technology. For example, Cold Snap frozen dessert mix was based on an innovative technology that enabled the consumer to make a frozen dessert that was meant to be an

ice cream replacement. In hindsight, it was a flawed idea
and should have been killed long before it was. As one former P&G brand manager explained it, "They were mesmer-
ized by the [technology of it]. They tried to persuade
consumers to eat the stuff, but it just was not a taste that
they liked. And it was a pain in the neck to make. But they
wouldn't let it die for the longest time." It was not an expensive mistake; the product never made it out of test marketing.

P&G's stumble in the soft drink market also provides insight into the company's focus on product technology.
Juelene Beck joined P&G in 1983, one year after P&G pur-
chased the Orange Crush brand. She was recruited from
Arthur D. Little, where she'd had some experience in the
food and beverage business. From her perspective, P&G
"was continually looking for technical superiority—to make
a better product and support advertising claims. They failed
to understand that the category was driven by image. For
fun and identity. Pepsi-Cola with Michael Jackson. Good-
looking young women. Kids identify with beautiful people
on the beach. We were trying to prove flavor superiority.
There was an amazing amount of not listening and not
hearing what was right in front of them. I felt they just
couldn't bear the fact that they wouldn't win through technical superiority." They sold their carbonated beverage
brands to Cadbury Schweppes.

Encaprin is another example. Encaprin was a brand of
analgesic that did not irritate the stomach because it was
based on time-release technology that allowed the product
to pass through the stomach before it dissolved. The analgesic was an ideal product for heavy users of aspirin—*if* the
product was taken every four hours. However, most people
don't take aspirin in anticipation of pain; they take aspirin
when the pain comes, and they want it to work right away.

P&G thought it could change consumer habits, especially with such an eloquent solution to such an important problem. With ibuprofens becoming a competitive factor, P&G didn't have time to waste with extensive testing. It skipped normal test-marketing procedures and introduced the analgesic nationally. The product was a relatively expensive failure.

But all these mistakes are more than offset by the successes that have resulted when P&G has persisted with new product technologies.

LESSON **10**

A product is only as good as it does.

Real value for the consumer in a product is a result of functional performance benefits—rather than benefits that are "cosmetic" or based on imagery.

P&G makes laundry products that get clothes clean, toothpaste that prevents cavities, shampoo that cleans and conditions at the same time, diapers that keep babies dry. In the lab, products are judged against the functional performance of competitive products. If a product is a new innovation, it is compared to whatever else is available to the consumer to meet that functional need (for example, when Pampers was first developed, it was judged against cloth diapers). If it is not measurably superior, it is not up to P&G standards. In marketing terms, "quality" is usually expressed as being superior to the competition.

When the product is no better than its competitors.

To underscore the importance of product performance to P&G, the story of Monchel, a brand of scallop-shaped soap developed in the 1980s, is recounted to P&G's trainees. It won in blind testing, but only because of its cosmetics—its unusual shape, fragrance, and package. The product worked no better than Lever Brothers' Dove soap. It was a failure, P&G concluded, because the company hadn't developed a product with superior performance.

When the "free" premium is more important than the product it comes with.

The P&G system is not geared for brands that exist for reasons other than product functionality. At one time P&G offered brands of detergents whose "reason for being" had nothing to do with their performance, but instead had to do with what *else* was in the box. Duz and Bonus were so-called premium brands—not because the brands were of premium quality, but because they came with a "premium"—Duz detergent had a "free" glass or dish, and Bonus detergent had a free dishcloth, washcloth, or towel, depending on the size package, inside every box. P&G marketed these brands to compete with competitive premium brands such as Lever's Breeze. The brands competed primarily on the basis of the consumer's preference for the design on the dish or the towels, not the quality of the detergent. Bill Cordes, a former member of the Bonus brand group, remembers that the brand had to be reinvented every eighteen months. The towel designs went through the same exhaustive testing that any other product modification would go through, and according to standard procedure, every time the package changed to display a new towel, it had to be reviewed by what was then called the administrative committee. It did not compete very effectively with Lever's Breeze. Lever could knock off P&G designs and move more quickly to the market. Neither P&G's expertise nor its careful procedures were suited to the marketing of dishcloth and towel designs. Bonus detergent and Duz detergent were withdrawn from the market in 1978.

When a pretty package is more important than the product.

P&G's marketing of a liquid hand soap product also illustrates its focus on product functionality. And, perhaps, reflects a lesson it had learned from Bonus detergent. P&G did not enter the liquid soap market until the early 1980s, when it had developed a product that not only cleaned hands but softened skin at the same time—a meaningful product difference. The brand group did its homework and, through consumer research, determined that what consumers wanted most in a liquid soap was not a soap that cleaned and softened skin at the same time but a pretty dispenser that eliminated the need for a messy soap dish in the bathroom and looked attractive to guests. The brand group hired an interior designer to develop package graphics that would complement the decor of the typical American bathroom. The product was blind-tested and was favorably received by the consumer, primarily because of the package.

The brand group named the product Rejoice and was ready to go to test market. When the package was reviewed by the CEO and the executive committee (the executive committee reviews *all* new or revised packages), John Smale, the CEO at the time, said, "Where's the logo?" When it was explained that a brand logo and positioning statement on the package would not, in the consumer's mind, enhance the decor of the bathroom, his response was, in effect, "We're in the business of providing superior products to the consumer—products with clearly distinguishable brand names and positionings. We're not building our business by competing on the basis of pretty packages."

The package was redesigned with a prominent logo and a design that was reminiscent of the Crest packaging. It failed in the test market. P&G could have reintroduced the brand with a pretty package, but it chose not to. True to its core values, it chose to compete on the basis of product performance, not package-design preference. The consumer would not accept the brand based on its product performance alone, and P&G refused to compete on the basis of package cosmetics.

This is not to say that P&G rejects style and imagery as marketing tools. But it does not start there. First the brand must provide a product performance benefit. That benefit is at the core of what the brand is all about and is integral to any style or imagery that is used to market the brand. This will be discussed further in Chapter 6.

LESSON **11** ——————————————

The best is never good enough.

Once you have improved a product, improve it again.

———————————————————————

You move ahead by being dissatisfied.
—**Neil McElroy, former P&G CEO**

The process never ends. Every P&G brand is continually improved. P&G has improved Tide detergent's product formulation and packaging more than seventy times.

P&G made history with Crest toothpaste several times. First with the first stannous fluoride toothpaste, in late 1955, then with sodium fluoride, an even more effective cavity fighter. Then, researchers took on the challenge of coming up with a tartar-control product. The difficulty was that tartar bonds to teeth in much the same way that fluoride interacts with teeth. So anything that worked on tartar worked against fluoride. P&G scientists discovered an anti-tartar ingredient, soluble pyrophosphate, that reduced tartar without affecting fluoride. The *Wall Street Journal* named Crest tartar-control toothpaste one of the "milestones of the decade." P&G licenses the ingredient to most of the major competitive brands.

CREATE UNIQUE BRANDS

What do the following names mean to you? Chevrolet, Marlboro, Coca-Cola, Avis, Sony, Anacin, Motorola, Timex, Nike, Listerine, Pepperidge Farm, Sears.

Chances are you know what product categories these brands are in and have an impression of how they differ from other brands. You also probably have some positive or negative feeling for each brand that goes beyond its basic product performance. P&G wants to make that same kind of connection to the consumer with all its brands.

LESSON **12** ————————————————————

Consumers buy products, but they choose brands.

Consumers form relationships with brands, not products, and not corporations. The performance of the product, what it does and how it does it, is the core identity of the brand. But the brand also has a distinctive personality and character that makes an emotional and trust-based connection with the consumer and distinguishes it from competitive brands.

Some companies *are* the brand—for example, Sony, Ford, Levi's, Hewlett-Packard, Apple, and Coca-Cola. Even packaged-goods companies occasionally lend their names to their brands (for example, Colgate toothpaste, Palmolive liquid detergent, Lever 2000 bar soap, Johnson's baby powder, Arm & Hammer toothpaste, Kellogg's corn flakes, Heinz ketchup, Hershey's chocolate bars, Gillette razors, Clorox bleach, and Campbell's soup). But P&G does not associate the name of the company with its brands. P&G will allow each new brand to say "New, from Procter & Gamble," but only for the first six months and only as a closing announcement in the advertising. After that, every P&G brand must stand on its own and make its own connection with the consumer.

The fact that every P&G brand is required to stand on its own reflects the company's fundamental belief in the uniqueness of individual brands and the importance of brands in establishing a bond of loyalty with the consumer. Ed Artzt, former CEO of P&G, has said, "Brand loyalty is the foundation of our business. A new mother has to decide what brand of diapers to buy every week. Most consumers buy a box of laundry detergent ten or twenty times a year. And every one of these purchase decisions is an opportunity to switch to another brand."

Brand equity is a matter of trust.

The relationship that consumers form with brands is often referred to as brand equity. Think of it this way: A mother is shopping for a toothpaste for her children and has a choice between two brands, both of which promise to reduce cavities. One is called Summit. The other is called Crest.

Chances are she is going to buy Crest toothpaste. She's never heard of Summit. Why should she believe Summit's promise? She has heard of Crest. It is comfortably familiar. She has heard about Crest's cavity prevention for years. She feels that the brand is kind of serious and no-nonsense about what it does, but also kind of friendly. It is a successful brand. Maybe she grew up using Crest herself. She *trusts* Crest. (All of that imagery is reflected in the current "I'm a Crest Kid" campaign, in which a very likable mother talks about growing up using Crest toothpaste and doing the right thing for her kids.)

Consumers form subjective attachments to brands and often exaggerate the real differences among them. It's not just a matter of trusting a familiar brand over an unknown brand. Consumers form exclusive relationships with brands that are impenetrable even by other well-known brands. A Crest loyalist won't buy Colgate toothpaste, and some even resent Colgate's competitive claims. Colgate loyalists feel the same way about Crest.

P&G is very protective of the equity of its brands. The

company is consistent in how it presents its brands to the consumer and has been very cautious about changing anything about the brand that the consumer has become familiar with—such as its logo, package design, colors, or flavors. For example, years ago, the company was very reluctant to add a mint-flavored version to complement the original wintergreen flavor of Crest. The brand group had test-marketed a mint-flavored version of Crest, a flavor similar to the original Colgate toothpaste flavor. Even though the test market resulted in significant sales-volume gains, Howard Morgens, P&G's CEO at the time, was concerned that it would "fuzzy up the image" of the brand. The mint-flavored version was not expanded out of the test market until it was finally concluded, several years later, that the original wintergreen flavor was not a defining element of the brand's identity.

LESSON **13** ————————————————

Be your own best enemy.

If someone's going to try to eat your lunch, better it be someone in your own family than an enemy. If there's room for more than one brand in a category, it's better to compete against one of your own brands than a brand from another company.

In the early 1920s when Lux, Palmolive, and Cashmere Bouquet soaps were introduced by P&G's competitors and began nicking away at Ivory's solid franchise, P&G introduced Camay, a hard-milled, perfumed toilet soap developed to outperform those competitors. The company's management was disappointed in the initial market performance of Camay. It didn't put much of a dent in the sales of Lux, Palmolive, and Cashmere Bouquet, which continued to thrive at Ivory's expense. In fact, management concluded that Camay had been held back by "too much Ivory thinking" and was not competing effectively because it was not allowed to compete head-to-head with Ivory. The eventual result was the creation of the brand management system, which gave each brand its own proponent within the company. *Time* magazine called it "a free-for-all among P&G brands, with no holds barred."

It's not quite a free-for-all. P&G brands are not so similar that they compete with each other for exactly the same consumers. P&G brands have different performance characteristics and provide distinguishable consumer benefits—even if they are only secondary consumer benefits.

For example, when Tide was introduced as the first "heavy duty" synthetic detergent in 1946, it was claimed to be the most effective detergent in the marketplace—which it was, by a significant margin. Soon, other synthetic detergents came on the market to compete. Some were intended to compete head-to-head with Tide. Others were positioned with benefits that were *in addition to* plain old straightforward heavy-duty cleaning, such as cleaning *and* whitening. Other brands were positioned for a somewhat different type of cleaning, such as cleaning delicate fabrics. All these brands compete with one another around the edges, but they stand for different primary benefits. P&G understands this and has often been the first to introduce separate brands that offer the consumer a choice. P&G has eight different laundry detergent brands in the U.S., including:

Tide—*if it's gotta be clean, it's gotta be Tide*
Cheer—*keeps colors bright*
Bold—*softens as it cleans*
Gain—*freshens as it cleans*

Era—*the power tool for stains*
Oxydol—*whitens as it cleans*
Ivory Snow—*for delicate fabrics*
Dreft—*won't irritate baby's tender skin*

P&G also has six bar soap brands, four shampoo brands, three light-duty liquid detergent brands, three toothpaste brands, and two fabric-softener brands. As long as each brand is positioned for a legitimate and distinctive consumer benefit, P&G will let it be an honest fight in the marketplace. P&G lets the *consumer,* not company management, decide which brand will succeed. P&G would rather that one of its own brands "cannibalize" one of its other brands than allow the competition to take share of market from the company.

When P&G pulls its punches, the competition steps in.

But it is not easy to maintain the discipline of internal competition, and even P&G breaks its own rules on occasion. For example, P&G's Pampers brand essentially "owned" the disposable diaper category with a seventy percent share of market in the late 1970s. When some competitors introduced an elastic-leg diaper, P&G introduced its own elastic-leg diaper—a brand called Luvs. However, P&G seemed quite protective of Pampers and avoided promising in advertising that Luvs provided a product benefit that would imply a deficiency in Pampers. The company positioned Luvs as a product providing an emotional end-benefit for the mother who by using Luvs does something extra for her baby—"Comfort your baby with Luvs"— because the soft, gentle gathers at the leg cradled the baby in a soft absorbent diaper. Unlike typical P&G TV commercials, no problem was set up to be solved and there was no demonstration versus the leading brand. The advertising wasn't very effective.

Kimberly-Clark's Huggies disposable diapers had at first made little headway in the Pampers-dominated market-place. Consumer research made it very clear to Kimberly-Clark that while baby comfort was important, the most compelling reason to buy elastic-leg diapers was that they "helped stop leakage"—which regular disposable diapers did not. Huggies was reintroduced as *the* brand that "helped stop leakage." The commercial showed babies who were un-happy because they were wearing "a saggy diaper that leaks" that looked for all the world like a Pampers diaper. It then showed how happy the babies became when they were in a Huggies diaper with "soft, gentle elastic to help stop leaking." Huggies leapfrogged Luvs, became the number-one-selling elastic-leg diaper, and took market share from Pampers that undoubtedly Luvs could have gained had P&G not broken its own rules of engagement.

LESSON 14 ─────────────

Gorilla brands are better than guerrilla brands.

Gorilla brands that dominate their categories realize efficiencies and economies of scale that give them a significant competitive advantage over their smaller competitors—not only economies of mass production but of marketing and advertising.

Brand dominance is an important principle at P&G. The company's emphasis is on volume and market share rather than on profitability. Because, ultimately, the dominant, high-volume brands are the more profitable brands.

Usually, P&G's "gorilla" brands are not threatened by P&G's smaller brands in the same categories. Tide is not going to be knocked out of the number one spot by Cheer. Crest, Downy, and Ivory are not going to be overtaken by other P&G brands in the same categories. Rather, the smaller brands tend to compete with other competitive brands in subsegments of the categories. At least, that's the way it works in ideal circumstances.

But guerrilla brands—brands that occupy a niche within a category—can take a piece out of the gorilla brand if they offer benefits that the consumer can't get in the gorilla brand. In the case of Pampers described in the preceding lesson, some Pampers users liked the idea of the elastic-leg diaper, but they couldn't get an elastic-leg diaper from Pampers. So they switched to Huggies.

The megabrand strategy.

The Pampers experience probably had something to do with an increased emphasis on the importance of building gorilla brands at P&G. The company calls it the megabrand strategy. The basic idea is to give the major P&G brands every opportunity to become as large as they can possibly become.

P&G no longer withholds the benefit of any major new technology from its major brands—as long as that technology is compatible with the brand's fundamental positioning. Ed Artzt explained several years ago, "We trapped ourselves, at times, into thinking that the best way to bring new technology to the market was to bring it out as a second brand. But you don't deny it to your market leader, or you are going to lose market leadership." Pampers now has an elastic-leg product in its line.

Similarly, the shampoo-and-conditioner "2-in-1" technology has been adapted to P&G's major shampoo brands. At first, P&G wasn't convinced that it was a broadly appealing technology. When it was first developed, it was added to Pert, a small and declining brand which was relaunched as Pert Plus. P&G was surprised when Pert Plus became a huge hit in the U.S. So the technology was added to Pantene shampoo in Taiwan, which enjoyed similar success. It was subsequently added to the Pantene brand around the world. Finally, eight years after it was first introduced with Pert Plus, the company decided to add the technology to Head & Shoulders shampoo. It has been a major boost for the brand around the world, and P&G has now concluded it should never have denied the technology to Head & Shoulders.

LESSON **15** ────────────────────

Expand the benefit, but don't compromise the brand.

The key to the megabrand strategy is to avoid incorporating new technologies into a brand, or extending its line, in a way that contradicts the brand's core positioning—its fundamental benefit and how the consumer thinks about the brand.

───────────────────────────

P&G has demonstrated on two occasions that it will not compromise Tide's heavy-duty-cleaning positioning—even if this results in lost sales. First, when P&G refused to market an inferior nonphosphate product, as its competition did, in the wake of a controversy in the 1960s over the use of phosphate builders in detergents (which is discussed in

Lesson #41). Then in the early 1980s, when liquid detergents were becoming popular. Liquid detergents provided a handy way to pretreat laundry (for example, Wisk around the collar). But they weren't as effective as powdered detergents for really tough regular laundry cleaning. P&G introduced a separate brand, Era, to compete with other liquid detergents. But it refused to add a liquid version of Tide until years later, when P&G was finally successful in developing a liquid formulation that would perform as well as Tide powder. P&G has also expanded the performance capabilities of Tide to include versions of the brand such as Tide with "bleach alternative" and Tide with color brighteners, as well as producing Tide with a variety of fragrances. None of these versions conflict with the brand's heavy-duty-cleaning positioning.

The addition of the "2-in-1" technology to Pantene shampoo and Head & Shoulders shampoo was successful because it expanded the benefits of using those brands without conflicting with the dandruff-prevention positioning of Head & Shoulders shampoo or the healthy, shiny hair positioning of Pantene.

However, the "2-in-1" technology was not compatible with the Prell shampoo brand. Prell was a forty-five-year-old brand that wasn't going anywhere fast when P&G decided to add the "2-in-1" technology to it to give the brand a boost. It didn't work. Prell users liked the product the way it was—basically a surfactant that got hair squeaky clean. The "2-in-1" technology made hair less squeaky. The loss of loyal Prell users more than offset any new users that the new formulation attracted to the brand. P&G went back to the old formulation and stemmed the decline.

————————————————————

Manage each brand as a separate business.

The brand management organization assures that the company's resources are focused to nurture and protect its brands.

———————————————————————————————

When a P&G product emerges from the research and development department and is ready to be marketed as a brand, it is assigned to a brand manager. At that point the brand manager and the brand group, led by the brand manager, are the focus for everything relating to that brand and its well-being—especially its relationship with the consumer.

Recruiting materials entreating college and business-school graduates to join the brand management organization show a diagram of a wheel with the brand manager at the hub of the wheel and product development, R&D, package design, market research, customer business development team (sales), TV commercial production, promotion support, and all the other "departments" as spokes in the wheel. However, the departments do not report to the brand manager. They report up their own chains of command to the senior-vice-president level, and the brand manager has no real authority over them. Nevertheless, the brand manager is in the center of all the action affecting his or her brand, and the company looks to the brand manager to earn the goodwill of the departments and provide leadership to drive the business forward.

In fact, an important part of the brand manager's success depends on his or her ability to compete effectively for the attention and resources of these departments. The marketing manager and category manager (the brand manager's chain of command) make sure the competition among the brand managers does not become counterproductive for the category and for the company. They also make sure that each brand has a distinctive positioning and has access to technology developments appropriate for each brand. Thus, some of the rough edges in the competition among brands are rounded off. Still, each brand must stand on its own and deliver business results that merit the company's investment and support.

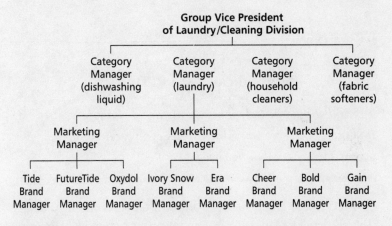

The importance of the brand and the brand management system is underscored by the fact that every P&G CEO has come up through the brand management ranks since the system was put in place in 1931. All of the company's current top management—the chairman and CEO, the president and COO, and all four executive vice presidents—were once brand managers.

MAINTAIN A LONG-TERM VIEW

The successful companies in James Collins and Jerry Porras's book *Built to Last* all have one thing in common—a long-term view. That doesn't mean that excellent companies do not make short-term adjustments to the marketplace. But their core values and principles are constant and focused on the long-term health of the enterprise. Said another way, if you don't have a vision of where you are going—and why—you'll never get there.

LESSON **17**

A brand can't stand still.

A brand should be a dynamic, constantly changing entity. It should evolve as consumer needs evolve, changing the way it satisfies consumer needs.

P&G doesn't believe in product life cycles. Its brands are not allowed to "mature," that is, after a period of growth settle into a stabilized marketplace and then eventually die. P&G builds brands that are intended to last forever.

Tide, for example, has evolved not only with improvements in basic technology but also in response to the way consumer needs have evolved. Over the years, washing machines have changed. Laundry habits have changed. Fabrics and lifestyles have changed. These changes have spawned new brands that have segmented the market. But they also have encouraged the expansion of the way the Tide brand has met its consumers' needs.

In the 1950s, for example, white cotton was the predominant fabric. So P&G improved Tide's whitening power with fluorescers. In the 1960s and 1970s, brighter colors and synthetic fabrics became more popular—producing clothes that were tougher to clean. An "Extra Action" Tide was introduced with new technology that increased soil removal for all kinds of clothing. Then, with a product formulation triumph, a liquid version of Tide was introduced in 1984. The fact that this new version has become the best-selling form of Tide in less than twenty years attests to the dynamic vitality of one of the oldest brands in the P&G stable. And although the product and packaging has changed in significant ways over the years, it's still the same *brand* it was fifty years ago. Its advertising strategy is unchanged; it is still positioned as the brand that "gets clothes cleaner than any other product you can buy."

P&G continuously evolves its brands—by improving their performance or adding functionality to develop megabrands. With Crest, for example, the development of tartar-control technology was a major achievement and added contemporary vitality to the brand in an important way. Tartar prevention and gum care had been gaining public awareness, and the therapeutic benefits of cavity prevention and tartar control are very compatible. P&G also evolved the brand with different product forms, such as gels and pump dispensers.

P&G is not always in the lead with new product formulation. P&G was reluctant at first to incorporate whitening and brightening peroxide and baking soda ingredients into the Crest brand when line extensions of Colgate, Mentadent, and Aquafresh were introduced. The functionality of those ingredients were certainly not in the same league as

the therapeutic cavity prevention and tartar control technologies that Crest had pioneered. Nevertheless, the consumer made it clear she wanted those benefits, and the
Crest brand now includes a "multi-care" line extension, a
foaming toothpaste with baking soda, to keep the brand
contemporary and to be responsive to consumer wants.

LESSON **18** ————————————————————

Promote from within.

*The promote-from-within policy develops long-term
employees. Since each generation of future management
must come from within, this results in a self-imposed
discipline of hiring the best people the company can find,
then developing them to become the best they can be.*

The promote-from-within policy at P&G puts pressure
on the company to recruit effectively, to give its future managers intensive training and a comprehensive range of
experiences, to build an ongoing evaluation-mentoring-
coaching process into the system, and to provide attractive
career opportunities so that the company can keep the people it wants to keep. The development of subordinates is
taken very seriously and is a critically important part of
every supervisor's job.

A former P&G personnel manager gained an apprecia-
tion for the policy when he had the opportunity to compare
the effects of P&G's one hundred percent promote-from-
within policy with the effects of the seventy-five percent

promote-from-within policy of Richardson-Vicks, a P&G acquisition in 1985. Although Richardson-Vicks was regarded as having an effective organization with values that were compatible with P&G's values, the seventy-five percent promote-from-within policy did not put the same kind of pressure on the system to develop its own people that P&G's policy did. There was an escape valve when it came time to fill a position. If no internal candidate "was ready," they could still go outside to fill the position. They could even miss the seventy-five percent target if necessary. There simply was not the same sense of purpose applied to the staff development process as there is at P&G.

LESSON **19** ————————————————

Build enduring company-to-company relationships.

Outside organizations can make important contributions to a company's success. They should be nurtured.

As P&G builds long-term, trust-based relationships with its employees, so too does it build long-term, trust-based relationships with outside organizations.

P&G values its relationships with outside organizations, such as its advertising agencies, suppliers of raw materials, package design consultants, research suppliers, and even the academic community. Its collaborative relationship with Indiana University resulted in the discovery of a stannous fluoride toothpaste that reduced tooth decay. And its collaborative relationship with an enzyme supplier resulted in the invention of the "Carezyme" enzyme in Tide and Cheer that keeps clothes looking bright. It is a proprietary technology that the supplier shares exclusively with P&G.

P&G values the knowledge and resourcefulness of its suppliers, the experience of its consultants, and the creative capabilities of its advertising agencies and package design consultants. It has no interest in taking those functions "in house." The company realizes that to take away these organizations' independence could be stifling, and it values the experience that is acquired as these organizations work with a range of other clients.

Advertising agencies are full partners.

One of the best examples of P&G's long-term relationships is the partnership formed with its advertising agencies. The importance P&G places on the partnership reflects the importance of advertising in building brand equities and a strong relationship between the brand and the consumer. P&G believes that great advertising grows out of a thorough understanding of the brand and the marketing environment. The company involves its agencies in all aspects of its business and counts on them for their strategic thinking as well as the advertising that results.

Many companies are quick to fire their advertising agency when sales are not meeting expectations or when a new marketing director wants to "take a fresh look" at the advertising or "have his own team." P&G does not change agencies for any of these reasons. It *has* changed agencies in the past when sales were not satisfactory, but P&G learned that not only was changing agencies disruptive and inefficient, it was usually a cop-out. The problem was seldom one for which the agency was totally at fault or that the agency was incapable of fixing. And it was seldom just an advertising problem. As often as not, as was the case when Pringles was switched to another agency, the problem involved the product itself and not only the advertising. Just as P&G managers share the responsibility for the performance of their subordinates, the company shares the responsibility for getting great advertising from its agencies.

P&G's agency relationships last a long time. More than eighty percent of its advertising spending is handled by agencies that have been with P&G for thirty-five years or more. P&G values these relationships and works at maintaining them. It regards these relationships as collaborative partnerships committed to P&G's strategic goals. This commitment prohibits the agencies from working on any competitive accounts. In return, P&G has a sense of loyalty toward its agencies and seeks to assure that they are successful and profitable.

P&G has added new agencies to its roster as a result of agency mergers or to keep its brands out of agencies that handle competitive brands. When P&G does seek to hire a new agency, it is looking for a partnership rather than an advertising campaign. Unlike most other companies, it doesn't ask the agencies it is considering to create speculative advertising. P&G knows that speculative advertising created in the short time frame of an agency review is hit or miss: the best advertising will not necessarily come from the best advertising agency. Rather, P&G asks the agencies to show work created for their other clients and to tell how it relates to the advertising strategy and how they got there. P&G is looking for the linkage between analytical thinking and creativity and the processes that make it work.

The new selling partnership.

P&G has also had long-standing relationships with the retail trade through which its products are sold to the consumer. But, historically, these have been adversarial vendor-retailer relationships in which P&G had tried (quite successfully, as described in Lesson #50) to gain leverage versus the competition. In the last ten years, P&G pioneered a partnership relationship with the retail trade by transforming its sales organization into customer business development teams. The customer business development teams comprise representatives of the product divisions, marketing, logistics, finance, and information technology. They work with their counterparts at the retailer account, and as a group, their mission is to find ways to build the business of *both* companies. Many of the teams live and work together in the city where the account is headquartered.

LESSON **20** ────────────────────────

Build long-term profit.

Long-term survival depends on long-term profitability.

P&G is aggressive and unabashed about its pursuit of profits. The company believes that profitability is linked not only to the long-term interests of its employees, but also to the long-term interests of its consumers and the organizations the company does business with. Because, without profits, the company would cease to function.

Echoing Cooper Procter's statement in the 1880s about the "inseparability of interests" of the firm and its workers, former CEO Ed Harness had this to say in the late 1970s: "Procter & Gamble has succeeded throughout the 140 years since its founding for many reasons. Key among these is the fact that company management has consistently kept profit and growth objectives as first priorities. . . . Somehow our predecessors were wise enough to know that profitability and growth go hand in hand with fair treatment of employees, of customers, of consumers, and of the communities in which we operate."

The drive for profitability is not unique. What *is* unique is the long-term perspective that P&G has about profitability. P&G's management does not fret about quarter-by-quarter profits the way other companies' management does, and they don't devote a great deal of energy to holding the hands of stockholders and Wall Street analysts. P&G believes that profits will come as a result of good business decisions and good decisions have effects that last longer than a calendar quarter.

Over the years, P&G has made bold investments at the expense of short-term earnings. For example, when P&G developed a new synthetic detergent that became the Tide brand after World War II, the company was faced with a huge capital expenditure for continuous soap-making equipment that would render its soap-making kettles obsolete and seriously interrupt production of existing products. P&G decided to "mortgage the farm and go for broke," a phrase first used by Richard Deupree, P&G's CEO in the 1930s, and often repeated by P&G executives. In the course of the next decade, the company invested as much money in plant and equipment as it had in its first hundred years. Again, in 1984–85 P&G took a significant hit in earnings as a result of the installation of new disposable-diaper production lines around the world. This was a long-term strategic investment that paid off, but years later.

The long-term perspective on profit is why P&G got into pharmaceuticals even though development costs are high in that industry and lead times range from indefinite to for-

ever. P&G got in because the pharmaceutical industry rewards innovation handsomely, and innovation *is* a P&G
strength.

The long-term perspective on profit is also why P&G in-
vests to build dominant brands; they require a heavy up-
front investment and a long time to grow and mature, but
they're more profitable in the long run.

This perspective is also why P&G has taken short-term
write-offs on discontinued brands or divested itself of
brands that, although healthy, delivered below-average returns or didn't fit P&G's long-term strategic plans. P&G's
sale of the Duncan Hines line and its termination of a joint
venture marketing Aleve painkiller are recent examples.
These products did not fit P&G's strategic plan to develop
global brands.

P&G's long-term perspective comes more sharply into
focus when contrasted to the policies of companies that are
driven by short-term earnings and are less willing to invest
in the future. Colgate-Palmolive is a good example over the
years, according to these media comments:

> Turning out new products that succeed requires a finely
> tuned marketing machine. Colgate, [CEO George] Lesch
> found, simply did not have one after 22 years [1938–60]
> of [Edward] Little's rule. Lesch launched a crash pro-
> gram to create almost overnight what it had taken P&G
> 30 years to nurture and perfect.
>
> —*Forbes*, February 1, 1966.

> [CEO David] Foster, desperate to keep earnings rising,
> was cutting back on advertising and holding down on
> research and development spending—the lifeblood of
> any marketing company. In short, he was borrowing
> from the future with the hope that tomorrow would
> bring a stronger economy to bail him out.
>
> —*Fortune*, September 24, 1979.

[CEO Keith Crane] was also the prototypical Colgate boss, ruling with a stifling, autocratic hand. "The culture had always been closed," says a former company executive. "People had a very narrow vision of the future. After all his years at Colgate, Keith was not about to change the way they did business."

—*Fortune,* May 11, 1987

Wall Street likes companies that deliver steady profit increases and that are highly predictable. But P&G will sacrifice short-term increases for the sake of long-term opportunities, and the company is reluctant to explain its actions to Wall Street if doing so will reveal useful information to its competitors.

P&G has a long history of distancing itself from Wall Street. In fact, the company was delisted from the New York Stock Exchange for twenty-six years earlier in this century when it announced simply, "It is the opinion of the directors that the best interests of the company will be served by not giving out published statements. The earnings of the past year were in excess of the twelve percent dividend on the common stock. If you apply in person at the office of the company, you will be given more information if you desire." P&G was eventually relisted after it rescinded the policy of strict secrecy, but the company is still reluctant to appease the short-term Wall Street view. It's not that P&G management doesn't care about the price of its stock—especially since twenty-five percent of the stock is owned by P&G employees. Rather, it rests its case on its long-term growth and profit performance.

CHAPTER

2

THE P&G CULTURE

What is culture? Culture is an integrated set of beliefs, knowledge, rituals, and traditions. The strength of a company's corporate culture can have a significant effect on its performance, and there has been a growing awareness of this in academic circles and among those who study the factors that relate to business performance. For example:

In Search of Excellence in 1982 stated that "Without exception, the dominance and coherence of culture proved to be an essential quality of the excellent companies [we studied]." P&G was featured as an example.

Corporate Culture and Performance, published in 1992, employed a methodology of measuring corporate cultures. It concluded that P&G has an extraordinarily strong corporate culture. P&G's culture ranked *third* out of 202 companies studied—with a decidedly stronger culture than *any* of its competitors.

Built to Last, published in 1994 and updated in 1997, is a book about eighteen visionary companies—companies that over time have demonstrated resiliency, adaptability, and a very high degree of success. An important theme throughout the book is that a strong culture, supporting core ideologies, is a fundamental characteristic of visionary companies that differentiates them from their competitors. P&G is one of the visionary companies featured in the book.

The guiding principles in the preceding chapter provide direction for the business and are a foundational part of P&G's culture. This chapter explores some beliefs, values, practices, rituals, and corporate idiosyncrasies that support those principles. These have evolved over time and help characterize the company as it is today.

BELIEFS

LESSON **21** ————————————————

Do the Right Thing.

Doing the right thing is not always convenient. In fact, it is usually not the easy way out of a dilemma or the most politic thing to do. But doing the right thing is based on principle and is invariably best for all concerned over the long term.

There is no potential business gain, no matter how great, which can be used to justify a dishonest act. The ends cannot justify the means because unethical means, in and of themselves, can and will destroy an organization.

—**Owen Butler, former P&G chairman**

A principle isn't a principle unless it costs you something.

— Bob Goldstein, former P&G vice president, advertising

Do the Right Thing means do the ethical thing.

Ask any current or former P&G employee about P&G's ethics and you are likely to hear about the company's voluntary withdrawal of Rely tampons. When the incidence of toxic shock syndrome spiked in 1980, an all-out effort was launched to find the cause. Although the media and the Centers for Disease Control cited an apparent correlation of the disease to the use of Rely, a group of preeminent outside scientists, in a preliminary review of the data, concluded that there was no scientific evidence that Rely was the cause. P&G CEO Ed Harness asked this group of scientists, "Can you assure me there's no way Rely can be involved?" The answer was no, they couldn't, at least not until more was known about the disease. But that would take time. Harness's response was immediate. "Okay, we'll withdraw the product." The risk of Rely being a cause of the disease was too great; the treasured bond of trust the company had with the consumer was at stake.

FROM THE P&G BUSINESS CONDUCT MANUAL:

You should be able to answer "yes" to the following questions before taking action:

Is my action the right thing to do internally?

Would my action withstand public scrutiny?

Will my action protect P&G's reputation as an ethical company?

If your answers are not an unqualified "yes," don't do it.

Fewer people know about a less dramatic, but no less telling, example of Doing the Right Thing that was related to the Rely incident. When P&G withdrew the brand from the marketplace and terminated all advertising, P&G executives went to DMB&B, its advertising agency for Rely, and offered compensation. DMB&B had been counting on the commissions from national advertising for Rely to compensate it for its investment during the development and test-market phases. The agency had worked hard in good faith, and P&G felt it should not be penalized by the company's decision. This was more than a gesture. Even when the agency refused the offer, P&G insisted. It was the right thing to do.

Jim Schadt recalls another instance of P&G Doing the Right Thing. When Schadt was running Cadbury Schweppes Foods Ltd. in 1989, he bought the Orange Crush and Hires brands from P&G. Six months later, Ed Rider, who manages the P&G archives, delivered a package to Schadt containing two original Norman Rockwell paintings of little girls holding Orange Crush bottles. P&G had received the paintings when it bought the Orange Crush company and had forgotten about them when it was negotiating the recent sale. Schadt said, "They felt that the paintings were logically a part of the Orange Crush assets. They could have kept them, but they were so dreadfully honest that they gave them to us at no cost."

Do the Right Thing means be objective and true to the facts.

It is not easy to be objective and true to the facts. When former P&G brand-management people are first exposed to the real world outside of P&G, they are disturbed to see how readily people hear what they want to hear or, worse, distort facts to support their point of view. P&G employees are not immune to this temptation, and there are stories of some ambitious brand managers at P&G who have knowingly distorted the facts to get approval for their recommendations. But the stories usually end with the recounting of the outrage that accompanied the discovery of the sin and the punishment of the culprit. It is not the norm at P&G.

In the view of a former researcher at Burke Marketing Research, there was a significant difference in this regard between P&G and other clients. Many clients typically expressed satisfaction or dissatisfaction with the research company's results depending on whether or not the results validated the client's opinion. Or clients sought to "steer" the data to support a desired conclusion. However, P&G clients, true to Dr. Smelser's legacy, seemed to care only about the accuracy and validity of the data. They seemed to treasure the results—*whatever* they were. The best answer is whatever the facts say the answer is. Then they would take appropriate action on the basis of the findings. Doing the Right Thing is doing whatever careful analysis dictates.

Do the Right Thing means do what is best for the business long-term.

Gary Stibel was on a fast track and had just been promoted to brand manager of Duncan Hines ready-to-spread frosting. The brand was a blind-test winner versus the General Mills product, a pilot plant was built to manufacture test-market quantities of product, and high-scoring advertising had been produced. It was ready to go into test market.

After thirty days on the brand, Stibel prepared a recommendation to kill the brand. He had concluded that it was too small for the Procter system. It could not justify the expense of standard P&G test marketing, and even if it did go into test market, previous experience competing with General Mills indicated it was highly likely that that competitor would preempt a national introduction. Unless the company was prepared to forgo test marketing, reduce overhead, and take the brand national as a line extension, it was in the best interest of the company to discontinue the brand.

Stibel's boss disagreed and suggested that such a recommendation from a new brand manager would be suicidal. But when Stibel insisted, his boss agreed to forward the recommendation with his dissenting opinion in a cover memo. The advertising manager, two levels above Stibel, also dissented but forwarded the memo. But the division manager agreed with the analysis and approved the recommendation to close down the brand. He personally congratulated Stibel for Doing the Right Thing. Stibel was promoted to brand manager of New Products, Food Division, responsible for five brands.

LESSON 22

Strategic thinking is a way of life.

Strategic thinking is an information-based approach to leveraging assets and competitive strengths to achieve a result that aligns with long-term goals.

Former P&G assistant brand manager Cheryl Bachelder summed it up best: "I have the highest respect for P&G. Above all, for their strategic approach to everything— whether it's the way they approach the global marketplace as a corporation or the way they approach the consumer marketplace with a box of Biz all-fabric bleach. It's a discipline I have not seen replicated in the companies I've worked for since I've left. And I attribute a great deal of my personal success since I left to learning how to think strategically."

Another former P&G employee described it this way: "It was the best first job I could have had. I learned how to get things done with a purpose, thoroughness, and clearly defined goals. Establishing action plans, critical paths, and who needs to be involved. How to develop a marketing analysis and evaluate advertising based on what we're trying to accomplish rather than 'we have this idea' kind of thing. I spearheaded a process for people development for the company [that I work for now]—recruiting, interviewing, performance evaluations, and promoting from within if possible. All with a clear sense of purpose. It makes so much sense if you know how to do it, and it's amazing how loose and ad hoc the thinking is in other organizations."

Former CEO Ed Artzt summarized the role of strategic thinking at P&G in a talk with graduate students at the Wharton School:

> Good strategic thinking comes more easily to some people than to others. It is an acquired skill, and it can be learned, but it takes enormous personal discipline. One of the reasons is that our instincts, and sometimes our convictions, are not always strategic. . . .
>
> It is easy for certain kinds of managers to formulate a losing strategy with great zeal. These are managers who have a superficial knowledge of the facts of their business, a misguided view of the strength of their competition, or a limited understanding of the options available to them.
>
> Strategic planning is a complex process designed to

P&G Strategic Thought Model

SET OBJECTIVES ⇨	DIVERGE AND LEARN ⇨	REVIEW KEY FINDINGS ⇨	CONVERGE AND LEARN ⇨	EVALUATE OPTIONS ⇨	RECOMMEND ACTION
Objectives:	Review Bounty business in West Coast region:	• Weakness traced to the S. California districts.	• Conduct focus groups, ethnographic study, to seek opportunities to grow the Hispanic market. Consider targeted copy, media, or promotion.	• Review past experiences of other brands.	• Show how recommended actions address immediate and long-term strategic objectives of Bounty brand and Paper Division.
Improve Bounty towels performance in West Coast market	• Share and shipments: is the problem endemic to the region, or can it be isolated?	• Significant increase in ScotTowels trade promotion throughout the West Coast region.		• Talk with Sales, Hispanic marketing consultants.	
Rationale:	• Competitive review:	• ScotTowels heavily merchandised in channel serving S. California.	• Work with Sales Department and Promotion Department to develop merchandising programs that appeal to the customers of the mass merchandisers.	• Cost-benefit analyses of options.	• Provide basis for confidence that plan will succeed.
• West Coast is an important growth market for Bounty.	—product mix —advertising —media —promotion —pricing	• Bounty loyalty is weak in the Hispanic community.			• Measurements, criteria for success, and cost justification.
• Sales and share of market are falling behind objective.	• Distribution channels analysis	• Store checks and retailer visits indicate Bounty out-of-stock situation in retail channels serving Hispanic communities.			• Next steps and follow-up.
• West Coast is a strategic market for the Paper Division.	• Review Consumer Tracking Study.				
	Seek other ideas:				
	• Sales Department.				
	• Conduct store checks.				
	• Retailer visits.				
	• Focus groups				

determine the direction a company or business will take, where it wants to end up and how it intends to get there. By its very definition, strategic planning is a selective process. You make choices from options developed within a variety of feasible scenarios. . . .

It's all about winning. It's all about gaining competitive advantage through reallocating resources, deploying innovations, avoiding doing the same thing on the same battleground as the competition, and gaining advantage through measures competitors will find hard to follow. . . .

My advice is to train yourself to think strategically about every important decision in your life. There is no better way to practice the art of strategic thinking than on yourself. And it is fun sometimes. Try to think strategically about your career plan, about your free time, about your finances, your civic or volunteer activities, even your social life. In other words, the things you think about a lot.

LESSON 23

Winning is everything.

Winning is not just beating the competition. It's also achieving your own goals and beating your own benchmarks. It's being the best you can be. Winning is growing.

At P&G, winning is an attitude toward work—and a way of life.

On a corporate level, winning means finding the product innovations and improvements that will keep you ahead of the competition. And, if you already have the lead, the best way to stay ahead of the competition is not to coast while they catch up, but to improve upon your own best efforts. Winning also means understanding the consumer and the competitive environment and marketing those innovations and improvements in an intelligent, strategic way.

On a personal level, winning doesn't mean the other guy has to lose. As former P&G brand manager Bruce Miller put it, "It's not a zero-sum game. It's more like golf than tennis. You are playing against yourself and the course, not the guy across the net or in the next office. Play your best game and, if it's good enough, you'll be a winner. You might not achieve the specific goal you have set, but the company is big enough and flexible enough to move you up and onward in a way that suits your talents. That's winning."

Miller remembers the story of an assistant brand manager who, by his own account, was achieving great things and looked as if "he had the world by the tail." At about the time his "class" was ready to go out on sales training, he had a closed-door meeting with his boss. His peers assumed he was the first to get the nod. It turned out his performance had all along been more flash than substance, and the meeting with his boss was to discuss other career alternatives inside or outside the company. Miller is convinced that the moral of the story is that winning is all about your own performance and results and *not* about keeping up with what the other guy *seems* to be doing.

Former CEO Ed Artzt equates winning with professionalism:

It's mastery of the fundamentals. And that's what you must do to win in management. You must master the fundamentals of the business you're in, the functions you perform, and the process of managing people. If you don't do that, you'll eventually become a journeyman or journeywoman, and the brilliance you once had will surely tarnish.

Mastering the fundamentals of any profession, be it in the arts, sports, or business, requires great sacrifice, endless repetition, and a constant search for the best way to do things. . . . A professional in search of mastery brings an attitude to his or her work that no sacrifice is too great, and no experience or grunt work too menial if it helps achieve mastery of the fundamentals. . . . It all begins with attitude, striving to attain professionalism and embracing winning as a way of life. . . . If you want to become a winning manager, I urge you to embrace that attitude with all your might.

LESSON **24**

Know all that is knowable.

Knowledge is the foundation of strategic thinking and the basis for all decisions. It is the basis of winning.

The ability to retain and synthesize data, facts, and knowledge is an important performance criterion at P&G. Before they are hired, brand-management candidates are tested for their awareness of, curiosity about, and retention of details about generally knowable information. Once hired, they are expected to know key data and information related to their brands and to readily contribute them to any discussion: customer orders, shipment data, market share, business performance by region, competitive activity, demographic trends, key consumer research data and usage trends, media activity by market, and so on. Business discussions are typically very informative and data laden, and often the discussions will be stalled by a question until all the facts related to the question are ascertained.

LESSON **25** ————————————————

Find the action in the data.

Actionable implications can be found in regularly gathered marketing data, such as shipment reports or competitive-share information. But, most important, any new research or information should be pursued with an understanding **beforehand** *of how the information will be used.*

Diane Harris, a former P&G market research manager, believes that the up-front planning that goes into any research project has everything to do with the quality of the research output. The requests to activate a research project that the brand groups submitted to the market research department not only included a statement of objectives and a discussion of the issues but explicitly stated the *intended use* of the findings. "Everyone knew exactly what the project was all about and what it was intended to accomplish, and it made it a lot easier to design the research plan. Some less sophisticated companies don't have as thorough an up-front planning process, and a lot of their research winds up as fishing expeditions."

Rick Snyder, another former P&G market research manager, adds, "Every single piece of research had to be actionable or it didn't get done. And the policy was that every single piece of research went to John Smale [then CEO] with the brand manager's one-page summary and recommendation. What that did was keep people honest. And it didn't waste money on research that wasn't going to be used."

LESSON **26** ——————————————

Opinions don't count.

When decisions have to be made in the absence of facts, it's a mistake to confuse "gut feel" opinion, which is not actionable at P&G, and informed judgment.

> An opinion isn't worth a damn if facts can be ascertained.
>
> **—Richard Deupree, former P&G CEO**

> The prevailing attitude is that *what* is right is far more important than *who* is right. Facts, truth, logic have far more authority at P&G than any individual.
>
> **—Brad Butler, former P&G chairman**

New assistant brand managers quickly learn that "I think . . ." is not a good way to start a sentence. "The data suggests . . ." is usually a safe opener. Even "In my judgment . . ." will probably get a hearing, but that "judgment" had better be supported by some kind of past experience, precedent, or evidence of some sort. "Because I feel it in my bones . . ." doesn't fly.

LESSON **27** _____

Truth has its own rhythm and harmony.

Anecdotal evidence is about as actionable as a "gut feel"
opinion—it isn't. Nevertheless, the dissonant note can lead
to important insights.

Brand managers and even some top executives are constantly in the field checking stores, attending focus groups,
and chatting with consumers in grocery stores and even
with their spouses or friends and neighbors, seeking opinions and reactions to products. If their experience is not
consistent with the hard data, the hard data are often revis-
ited to understand why.

Personal experience counts too. One brand manager
brought home Cold Snap homemade frozen dessert to experience it in a home-use situation. She knew the brand had
a problem when her husband "wouldn't eat the stuff." The
product died soon thereafter.

LESSON **28** _____

Capitalize on your mistakes.

Progress is not always in a straight line. The trick is to
recognize a mistake and look at it in a new way.

A famous mistake is a cornerstone of P&G's history. In
1879 the ingredients of P&G's new white soap, which they

had just named Ivory, were mixed by mechanical devices called crutchers. The crutcher's arms revolved in the white mixture until an attendant decided by sight, smell, and even taste that it was thick enough to be poured into soap frames. There it would cool and harden into blocks of soap before being cut and packed. One morning the man who tended the steam-driven crutcher went off to lunch and forgot to stop the machine. When he returned, he stood appalled. The frothy, puffed-up mixture obviously had been stirred too long. His supervisor determined that no harm had been done, since the ingredients of the product were unaffected.

A month or so later, reorders began to arrive with some customers asking for "that soap that floats." The incident and the consumer interest in the buoyant, floating cake of soap was brought to management's attention and the manufacturing process was adopted. Floating Ivory became a consumer favorite and the foundation brand for the company. All because of a lunchtime mistake.

Olestra, the hoped-for "breakthrough technology," began as a breakthrough mistake. Years ago, P&G was trying to concoct an easily digestible fat that would help premature babies gain weight. But the researchers didn't succeed. All they could manage was a fatlike compound so chemically chunky that it passed through the body unabsorbed. Good for sales of disposable diapers maybe, but not good for helping premature babies gain weight. Rather than scrap the project, P&G was alert to the recent trends toward low-fat foods and snacks, and it redirected the objective of the project to develop a fat-substitute product. Olean is the result.

According to the book *Built to Last*, the ability to capitalize on mistakes is a characteristic of visionary companies. P&G tolerates mistakes as accidents or as by-products of its purposeful, strategic work process. And it capitalizes on them. Some other companies do more than simply tolerate mistakes. The authors were struck by how other companies had made some of their best moves not by detailed strategic planning but rather by experimentation and trial and error. The 3M company has even institutionalized an experimental process in which its researchers "try a lot of stuff and keep what works." As one former 3M CEO has said, "Our company has, indeed, stumbled onto some of its new products. But never forget that you can only stumble if you're moving."

LESSON 29

Keep commitments.

Making and meeting commitments is essential to the efficient functioning of an interdependent organization.

Commitments are a matter of integrity at P&G. They are not made offhandedly. They are taken very seriously.

There is a very strong sense of interdependence at P&G. Almost all decisions and activities involve different departments, functions, and a lot of people. There is a cultural expectation that commitments will be made and that they will be met. No one wants to be the weak link.

Action plans involving interdependent functions are often agreed to in meetings. Everyone knows the purpose of the meeting and is prepared to participate and make the necessary commitments. They come to the meeting knowing what they can and cannot do.

The meetings themselves start with the commitment of

being on time. In some companies, the senior person attending the meeting is so very busy on such very important business that he or she is invariably late. At P&G, if senior people commit to a meeting, they're there on time. The junior people notice and pick up the habit very quickly.

The meeting—which usually involves discussing issues and options—is an engaging process for all the participants because they know that everything is driving toward the end of the meeting. That's where the rubber meets the road: conclusion, action items, and next steps. Evasiveness or an "I'll try" isn't good enough. Unless someone has no control over the ability to deliver on a commitment by a certain date, a commitment is expected that all can count on. Overdelivery on the commitment is great. Underdelivery is failure. P&G CEO John Pepper likes to quote Bob Galvin, a former chairman of Motorola, explaining how his father exacted a similar commitment: "He treated me to the most demanding discipline. He trusted me."

Performance evaluations have the same kind of expectations. Once the subordinate and boss agree on business goals and personal development needs for the subordinate, a commitment is expected on the part of *both* the subordinate *and* the boss to do their parts to make it happen.

———————————————

God is in the details.

Competitive advantage often turns on consistency and attention to detail. Small mistakes can be symptomatic of carelessness.

————————————————————

> Sophisticated competition for millions of buying decisions makes vital the finding of the little extra to amplify the small difference and the avoidance of small mistakes.
>
> **—Ed Harness, former P&G CEO**

> You don't do things right once in a while. You do them right all the time.
>
> **—Vince Lombardi, former NFL coach**

At P&G, there's thorough or there's sloppy, and not much allowance for anything in between.

Paul Kadin remembers learning about attention to details as an assistant brand manager on Luvs. He was in charge of getting all the sales and merchandising materials produced and ready for a presentation to the sales department prior to the introduction of the brand in the Columbus, Ohio, region. "There were a hundred things—from the key-account presentation kits right down to the buttons for the aisle clerks. I had done a good job, but I forgot to bring the shelf card you would stick under the boxes of Luvs on the shelf. The meeting was a big success, and my boss was the only one who noticed that the shelf card was missing. Nevertheless, he jumped all over me and stayed on me for a week. You got it right if it's one hundred percent. That's the standard of the place."

LESSON 31 ────────────────────────

Think sideways.

Product innovations, new ideas, and new ways of doing things can come from lateral thinking and reapplying lessons learned in other areas.

P&G started out making soap and candles with tallow, lard stearin, and cottonseed oil. When the price of lard went up, P&G leveraged its experience with cottonseed oil to invent the first all-vegetable shortening. Then the company's experience with crushing cottonseeds readily translated to crushing peanuts for peanut butter, and, more important, the knowledge of crushing and pulp technologies led to the development of paper products.

Experience with soap making and detergents led to the study of calcium in water, which led to an understanding of the relationship of calcium and fluoride in water, which led to an understanding of how tooth decay could be prevented with toothpaste. Knowledge about teeth and calcium led to the study of bones and to the development of pharmaceuticals such as Didronel, a prescription drug for treating osteoporosis.

Even advertising ideas can be reapplied, and P&G has institutionalized the concept of "search and reapply." For example, they have a copy services department that analyzes competitive advertising around the world as well as P&G's own advertising. It is a resource the brand groups can use to understand what works and what doesn't and what techniques have been tried that might be useful. A recent example is the successful "Show and Smell Challenge" advertising campaign for Gain laundry detergent in the U.S. The concept was created in London for P&G's Daz detergent in the U.K. TV commercials show a roving news team "surprising" a housewife with a challenge to check how her laundry smells.

In an earlier analysis, it was concluded that a Comet cleanser commercial was particularly effective because in the side-by-side scrubbing demonstration the competitive cleanser was given the advantage of an "extra swipe," but the Comet cleanser still did the better job. Since then, countless competitive products have been granted the "extra swipe" advantage of P&G demonstrations. To no avail; the P&G product always wins.

The closing shot in Downy commercials shows the bottle bouncing in slow motion on a stack of towels. This is the prototype for the shampoo commercials showing flowing or "bouncing" hair in slow motion.

The Health Care Research Center institutionalizes sideways thinking.

Probably the best example of how P&G institutionalizes the cross-fertilization of ideas is the way the new (established in 1995) Health Care Research Center in Cincinnati serves as the hub of the company's global network of R&D facilities.

One of the most striking things at the center is the exhibit of photographs by aerial photographer Georg Gerster and micro photographer Manfred Kage. At first, it is difficult to tell whether you're looking at a volcano or a skin pore or a microscopic view of drying linseed oil or an aerial view of a river meeting the sea in Namibia. The exhibit is supposed to symbolize the center's theme of continuous discovery by thinking of things in new ways.

The Health Care Research Center building itself is designed to stimulate cross-fertilization and lateral thinking. The corridors are extra wide, and there are escalators, rather than elevators, between the floors. The reason: studies showed that employees gather more readily for informal discussions in wider hallways, and they talk more freely on escalators than in elevators. The laboratory and office spaces are open in order to foster collaboration and interaction. There are "huddle rooms" and conference rooms nearby. They also have "team rooms" to serve as war rooms for the "speed teams"—cross-functional teams put together to cut through sequential and procedural processes in order to drive specific products from idea to expansion. (Speed helps. P&G calculates it takes $359 million and twelve years to develop and market the average drug. That's more than $81,000 a day!)

Researchers in the Health Care Research Center are encouraged to interact with other researchers in the P&G empire. P&G has a database of the specialized knowledge and experience of its scientists and technologists in its R&D facilities around the world. And P&G has videoconferencing centers to enable face-to-face meetings whenever the need arises. Then there's a "Global R&D Monthly Reports" database that provides researchers with a means to monitor monthly reports of interest based on author, region, sector, category, specific technologies, or projects.

P&G's cure for peptic ulcers, Helidac, was a result of the kind of collaboration that P&G is encouraging. The initial idea came from one of P&G's prescription-drug researchers. She got together with the company's over-the-counter scientists working on Pepto-Bismol, and, together, they worked with an Australian researcher who had discovered the bacteria that causes peptic ulcers.

LESSON **32** ————————————————————————

Expect the unexpected.

Competitive urgency must be balanced with the need to
avoid costly mistakes.

————————————————————————

P&G is regarded as a very conservative company—
especially by its own brand managers, who are eager to
make things happen. But a long history of some painful lessons has reinforced P&G's long-term perspective and its disciplined use of procedures to reveal problems before
expensive commitments are made.

Shelf tests, ship tests, extended in-home-use tests are all
standard procedure at P&G because even after all the pre-
testing homework and product analysis, the unexpected can
happen.

For example, P&G's first entry in the dentifrice category
was a spin-off of the company's synthetic detergent technology—a liquid dentifrice called Teel. Teel was tested in use
by consumers. They liked it. It was agreeably flavored, at-
tractively colored, and had a presumed advantage over
other toothpastes because it contained no abrasives. Teel
moved into national distribution and was a major success.
For a while. Then sales began to slide. The mouth chemistry
of certain individuals, it seemed, caused a discolored dental
plaque to develop. The consumer tests had not been extensive enough to ferret out the problem. The product was
withdrawn from the market.

A more recent example in the dentifrice category validated the company's patience in applying its test procedures. A toothpaste called White Cap was developed that

not only had a "hot" taste to compete with Macleans and Ultra Brite, but also had stannous fluoride. It was well received by the consumer in concept tests and home-use tests, the advertising was tested and ready, and everything was set to go. But, to the chagrin and frustration of the brand group and the advertising agency, P&G procedures also called for extended shelf testing. This step revealed that the combination of ingredients that provided the performance benefits of the product also ate holes in the tube. The brand was killed.

RITUALS: MEMOS AND MEETINGS

LESSON **33** ─────────────────────────────

Nothing happens unless it's on paper.

The written memo is integral to the P&G culture. It is the vehicle for exchanging information and making decisions.

When an idea or recommendation is put in writing, it stands on its own merit, supported by the strength of the memo's analysis and critical thinking alone.

Nowhere in the company is memo writing taken more seriously than in the brand management organization, because most of the decisions made by management are based on the information and recommendations that come up through the brand management organization. These memos are critiqued to assure that the information is accurately and concisely reported. Memos must be revised if a sentence of six words can be expressed as clearly with five words, or if a table of the data can communicate more effectively than a verbal description, or if data can be more appropriately detailed in an exhibit rather than in the body of the memo, or if an adjective doesn't provide the precise expression desired. Misspelled words or columns of numbers that don't add up are taken as evidence of carelessness and are not tolerated. P&G brand people become uncannily adept at spotting typos or mathematical errors—first in their own memos, then in reviewing their subordinates' memos. Some who have left P&G for new careers are astonished at the relative laxity and sloppiness of memos in their new organizations.

There are two basic types of memos—information memos and recommendation memos. Information memos include research analyses, store check reports, sales and market share data summaries, competitive analyses, focus-group observations, status reports, and so forth.

However, the prototype P&G memo, and the most thoroughly scrutinized, is the recommendation. The recommendation must present a logically sequenced and airtight intellectual case for the recommendation. Any perceived flaw in logic, spurious information, or unsupported opinion is unmercifully challenged.

LESSON **34** ──────────────────────

The memo is a template for strategic thinking.

The memo demands analytical thinking that is not only thorough and clear but is also consonant with longer-term goals. The format of the P&G memo connects the proposal to its strategic underpinnings.

───────────────────────────────────

The basic components of a recommendation memo usually include:

Statement of Purpose
Background
Recommendation
Rationale
Discussion
Next Steps
Supporting Exhibits

The Statement of Purpose is usually an introductory sentence that succinctly states the purpose of the recommendation being made. (In the illustrative memo that follows, the incremental funding that would be required in the current fiscal year is also mentioned because it is an important part of the decision that is being requested.)

The Background section that comes next is a very important part of the P&G recommendation memo. Often the *most* important. Other companies tend to give it short shrift or ignore it altogether. At some companies, there may be less need for a Background section. For example, there may be a shorter chain of command reviewing the memo, and

ILLUSTRATIVE P&G MEMO

February 12, 1995

From: C. L. Decker
To: J. O. Doaks
Subject: <u>Bounty Towels West of Rockies Remedial Plan</u>

This recommends a plan to regenerate market share growth of Bounty towels in the West of Rockies (WOR) region and requests incremental funds of $150,000 be made available this fiscal year. Sales (Ms. Jane Doe) concurs with the recommended plan.

Background

- WOR is a strategic market for the Paper Division; shipment volume must be increased in this region to realize distribution and supply efficiencies. The Division is committed to a) accelerating the growth of key brands and b) demonstrating our determination to win in this market. WOR is relatively immature for the Division and is still dominated by competition.

- Bounty market share growth has been on target until the past four months (see Exhibit 1 for market share details and shipment data):

Share	JASO	NDJF	MAMJ	JASO	NDJF (proj.)
Objective	22.6	23.1	23.6	24.0	24.4
Actual	22.8	22.7	24.0	23.6	22.6
Index	(101)	(98)	(102)	(98)	(93)

- This weakness can be traced entirely to four S. California districts (details in Exhibit 2):

	NDJF Market Share			NDJF Bounty
	Bounty (IYA)	Brawny (IYA)	ScotTowels (IYA)	Shipments (IYA)
Total WOR Region (100%)	22.6 (99)	33.6 (97)	20.2 (109)	802MSU (105)
4 S. Calif districts (27%)	18.8 (87)	32.1 (94)	23.6 (117)	216MSU (94)
Balance of WOR (73%)	24.0 (104)	34.4 (98)	18.9 (104)	586MSU (110)

- Bounty performance in the four S. California districts suffers from an underdeveloped and weakening trade and consumer franchise in the Hispanic market—which is heavily concentrated in southern California. Merchandising tracking services indicate that ScotTowels trade promotions throughout the WOR have been particularly effective in the retail channels serving the Hispanic community and have adversely affected

Bounty (Exhibit 3). Store checks confirm this and indicate an increasing Bounty out-of-stock situation (Exhibit 4). Bounty is not achieving consumer acceptance in the Hispanic community, as shown below (details in Exhibit 5):

| | 10/94 Consumer Tracking Study | | |
| | "Excellent" Ratings (vs. 10/93 study) | | |
	Bounty	Brawny	ScotTowels
Hispanics in WOR region	29.6% (+0.5)	43.7% (+2.2)*	39.9% (+4.4)
Non-Hispanics in WOR region	46.4% (+7.8)	45.4% (−2.3)*	40.17% (+1.1)*

*not statistically significant at the 95% confidence level

Recommendation

An advertising and promotion effort targeting the Hispanic community and the retail channels serving those communities should be implemented immediately. The plan will cost $170,000 in FY 94/95 and $230,000 in FY 95/96. This translates to a $4 million working media and promotion program on a national basis. Except for the requested $150,000 this fiscal, the plan will be funded internally by reallocation of resources and anticipated incremental volume generated by the plan.

Rationale

- The current Bounty advertising campaign is not relevant to Hispanics. ARS testing of the "Family Reunion" commercial among Hispanics yielded weak Recall, Purchase Intention, and Engagingness scores (compared to scores for "Family Reunion" among non-Hispanics and relative to norms for other mainstream commercials tested among Hispanics). Subsequent one-on-one qualitative research among Hispanic consumers indicates that a) the presentation of Basic Bounty and Extra Strength Bounty in the same commercial causes some confusion and b) Hispanic consumers don't relate to the family situations presented. These deficiencies were corrected in new copy developed specifically for the Hispanic market. This advertising was produced in rough animatic form and exposed to Hispanic consumers in one-on-one testing and focus groups. It was clearly understood and perceived to be relevant and appealing. (See Exhibit 6.)

- Copy Services experience with eight other P&G brands indicates that commercials specifically produced to address the Hispanic market resulted in a two to four times improvement in copy test measures and significant business gains when deployed in the marketplace.

- <u>The retail trade is sensitive to the Hispanic market and responsive to marketers who specifically address that market.</u> The Hispanic market is very important to retailers in southern California. Sales (I. L. Sellum) advises that Wal-Mart, Lucky's, and Safeway have expressed concern about Bounty turnover and that we will soon be vulnerable to item discontinuances if there is no improvement. He believes that the trade would be highly supportive of a consumer advertising effort combined with consumer and trade promotion events to develop the Hispanic market.

- <u>The recommended program is projected to pay out in 28 months or less.</u> Assuming that the recommended program generates only enough volume to match the brand's business development in the balance of WOR, the effort would pay out in 28 months, versus taking no action and allowing a serious deterioration of distribution and sales. (See Exhibit 7.)

- <u>The program can be spun off in other Hispanic markets.</u> Radio and television commercials produced for the southern California market— and the materials to merchandise these efforts to the trade—will be used selectively in some of the other Hispanic markets outside California (e.g., Texas, New Mexico, and, possibly, New York City and southern Florida) thus prorating production costs and sharpening the focus of Bounty marketing efforts in those markets. Variations among the Hispanic regions within the U.S. will be taken into account.

Plan Details, Scheduling, and Next Steps

It is imperative that we present a plan of action to the trade as soon as possible in order to forestall discontinuances. With immediate approval of this recommendation, trade presentations would begin in late March, and the first flight of radio advertising would begin on April 15 followed by television advertising in early May. Selective door-to-door sampling would begin at the end of the first flight of advertising in June. Trial size display units would be in retail distribution at the same time. Plan details, scheduling, and next steps are presented in Exhibit 8.

May we have your agreement to proceed?

—C.L.D.

all concerned may be familiar with the issues. But at most companies, a weak Background section can be symptomatic of a superficial understanding of the issues.

The Background section of the P&G recommendation memo has two functions. First, it connects the issue that the memo is addressing to the strategic objectives of the brand or the company. Second, it sets up the problem that the recommendation is supposed to solve. Background sections get a lot of scrutiny at P&G. Sometimes the reader doesn't even get past the background. If he doesn't agree with the framing of the problem, the solution is irrelevant.

The next section, usually called simply Recommendation, proposes how to solve the problem described in the Background. This is followed by a Rationale section, which spells out the reasons for the recommendation. Next are whatever sections that are appropriate, such as Rationale or Discussion, to anticipate reader questions or reservations that have not already been addressed, discuss risk assessment or alternatives, or provide details of the recommendation. The final section is Next Steps, followed by the Supporting Exhibits.

The comprehensive memo is important for a company like P&G, which has so many activities going on at any one time for so many brands, and in which decisions are so driven by data and past experience as they relate to long-term strategies.

LESSON **35** _____

The memo exposes flawed thinking—or burnishes brilliant thinking.

The P&G memo is a logical, sequential way of presenting ideas, and since all P&G memos are written essentially the same way, the format is familiar and comfortable. This "comfort" is disrupted if the connections aren't made in the document. If the background doesn't lead naturally to the recommendation, or if the recommendation isn't supported by the rationale, flaws are exposed. However, if all the connections are made, the thinking is unassailable.

If a recommendation does not specifically solve the problem or advance the brand's strategic interests, it won't flow naturally from the background. If it has not been thought through, if the risks or other courses of action have not been considered, that will be exposed by the format of the memo.

But if all the dots connect, the thinking seems to flow naturally and gracefully. To P&G people, it can be a thing of beauty. And sometimes the memo itself gets more attention than the ideas it contains. Gene Plummez remembers, when he was an assistant account executive at the Dancer-Fitzgerald-Sample advertising agency, the brand manager called him up to compliment him on a memo he had written: "Instead of saying 'What a great idea,' he said, 'What a well-written memo!' That kind of struck home about the importance of the memo at Procter."

Gene went on to speculate that "P&G seems to have figured out that if you structure information certain ways, people will readily understand it, good ideas will emerge, and bad ideas will be exposed. I really think that is what has made them so successful. They make fewer mistakes because they find mistakes before they happen. They just have a higher batting average because of that."

LESSON **36** ─────────────────────

If you can learn to write a P&G memo, you can learn how to think.

One of the reasons some P&G people get so obsessive about memos is that they believe that a flawed memo can be symptomatic of a flawed intellect. People in brand management don't get promoted if they don't have good communication skills. And memo writing is the ultimate communication skill.

The memo is not only the basis for decisions and information exchange, it is also a primary teaching tool—to teach marketing people how to think. The memo-writing experience is a rude awakening for the Harvard MBA who graduated with honors in English from Princeton. He has been rewarded throughout his academic career for long, erudite dissertations. But, that's a different kind of writing. The purpose of the P&G memo is not to demonstrate how much the writer knows or how many relevant connections can be made. The purpose is to distill the writer's argument down to the key points and express them clearly, simply, and persuasively.

Good editing is good thinking.

> That acceptable third version does not spring full
> blown from a mind in control of everything. It is
> slowly uncovered as one does his spadework during
> the writing of the first two versions.
>
>   —James A. Michener, writer

It is a rare P&G memo that goes through only three revisions. For the assistant brand manager just starting out, fifteen to twenty rewrites of his or her first memos is about par. Even after the memo gets past the brand manager, a half dozen or more rewrites might be expected as the memo gets passed up the line, and back down again. Thus, even the brand manager, who has been writing memos for several years, continues to receive training on how the company's higher management thinks—and how to write to that thinking.

Many people think the memo rewriting process at P&G is excessive. But no one seems to regret having gone through it. Paul Kadin spent three years in brand management after receiving his MBA. His comments are typical: "Remarkably simple topics would be revised ten times by your boss before [the memo] would be worthy to send on. It was really a process to teach you how to think. At the time, it was painful. It seemed like a waste of time. In hindsight, it was the best thing that ever happened to me. I find myself now thinking in terms that I was taught to write in. The logic flow is even more important than the way in which it is expressed in words. [And there's an] economy of words when it comes to talking about a business issue and taking somebody through your thought process that is a direct reflection of that discipline."

In the editing process, sometimes the connections are revealed as weak. By going through the same process that the reader will be going through—relating the solution back to the problem, and the rationale to the solution, and the alternatives to the rationale—the recommendation can evolve, be strengthened or changed. A good idea can be made better, but a bad idea can be exposed and scrapped or transformed into a good idea through the editing process.

Managers up the line do the same thing. When P&G executives pick up a memo, typically they also pick up a pencil. They don't just make comments or note questions in the margins; they edit. Perhaps they will insert a sentence or some words to clarify a point; the author of the memo can later agree, disagree, or reedit. But reviewing the memo with a pencil is more than critiquing or responding to the memo. It is a process by which the reader interacts with and understands the thoughts presented.

The myth of the one-page memo.

The celebrated P&G one-page memo is a myth. Memos originated at the assistant-brand-manager or brand-manager level are typically three or four pages long. But they *are* concise. Extraneous words are excised, as are extraneous issues and valid but inconsequential arguments.

Cover notes, however, are almost always one page or less. Cover notes include a summary of the memo, then summaries of the summaries, that serve to forward the memo up the line. Even the stationery of the cover notes decreases in size relative to the seniority of the manager writing the cover note. It is a very efficient method of communication in which each manager provides only as much information as is deemed appropriate for the next person up the line. But the original memo is attached if the person at the end of the line wants to read it.

LETTERS TO MAMA

A sequence of "letters to Mama," supposedly from a recently arrived assistant brand manager, spoofs the P&G memo and has been widely circulated within the company. The letters progressively conform to the P&G format.

BEFORE

Dear Mama,

    Well, here I am in Cincinnatti. I'm not sure if that's spelled right, with the two t's at the end. Spelling was never my long suit. Numbers, either.

    Tomorrow is my first day with Proctor & Gamble. . . . I imagine that with my business school background it will be a real snap. I can hardly wait to see which of their little companies I am going to be president of.

    I'm not staying at the hotel they had me in for the interviews, Mama. They said I would have to get my own place. No one took me out to dinner either. Clearly an oversight on *some*one's part. I bet they really catch it for that!

Your loving son,

Harold

AFTER

FROM: Harold

TO: Mama

SUBJECT: PERSONAL PROGRESS

This is to bring you up to date on recent developments in my life.

BACKGROUND: Approximately 24 years after you gave birth to me, I began working for P&G. Since then, I have been accumulating 3.2 new experiences per day (index of 670 vs. year ago).

CURRENT STATUS:

1. Health: Tired, but good.

2. Social Activities: Down 50% vs. previous week.

3. Memo Writing: My Brand Manager says I'm starting to get the idea.

NEXT STEPS: Write soon.

—HJM

LESSON **37** ─────────────────────────

A good memo is transparent.

Although the memo gets a great deal of attention, a good memo doesn't call attention to itself. The best memos are simple and straightforward and get out of the way of the ideas that they put forth. The ideas seem to stand alone in the mind of the reader.

───

P&G people are taught to write the way they talk; it tends to make the writing more conversational, accessible, and engaging. In the old days, they were encouraged to dictate their first drafts. Today most people who have recently joined P&G type their own memos. They are proficient with the word processor and have a conversational style on the keyboard bred by years of writing informal E-mails and having chat room conversations. After the first drafts, the editing process is intended to achieve conciseness without becoming so condensed that the conversational style is lost.

The key is to engage the reader's brain. Memos, like any kind of effective communication, must tap into the reader's predispositions or provide background information that can be readily understood and accepted. Questions or reservations should be addressed almost as they occur in the mind of the reader. The goal is to get the reader to nod his or her way through the memo. The ideas should flow naturally, as though they were the thoughts of the reader.

Tom Weigman remembers when he first realized the importance of connecting with the reader. As an assistant brand manager at the time, he was having a conversation over a beer with some of his peers about a memo that one of them was working on and the question came up of the best way to phrase a particular sentence in the memo. As Weigman related the story: "At that point, Bruce Miller said 'Wait a minute. Gary would do it this way,' and he would mimic the sentence the way Gary Stibel, a brand manager, would write the sentence. Then he mimicked the way two other brand managers in the division would write the sentence. And he had those guys absolutely nailed. He could mimic their style of writing. Now, you have to realize that Bruce was the hottest assistant brand manager in our class. He wrote exceptionally well. So we realized that when he worked for anybody, he wrote the memo just the way his boss would write it. So the boss would say, 'My God, this is perfect!' Because that's exactly the way he would write it!"

LESSON **38** ————————————————————

When a meeting is absolutely necessary, handle it like a memo.

There aren't many meetings at P&G—at least not as compared to other companies. Meetings are generally regarded as a relatively inefficient and ineffective way to exchange information or make decisions.

Meetings can be useful to "brainstorm," or to finalize decisions and next steps, or to exchange information and coordinate the efforts of an interdepartmental team. But these meetings are more purposeful and organized than those you might expect to see in other companies. Just as a well-crafted memo can be an extraordinarily effective tool for communicating information and recommending or initiating action, the same principles of organization and conciseness apply to the orchestration of a meeting.

The prevalence of meetings—and the lack of written communications—is a major adjustment for people brought up in the Procter & Gamble culture when they leave and join other organizations. With a memo, they can study the document to see that all the pieces fit. It's hard to see that in a meeting. Ex-P&G people also feel that the format of a presentation—from the graphics displayed to the presenter's style—can be distracting.

The creative review meeting, in which an advertising agency presents new advertising to a brand group, illustrates how the P&G meeting format works. Like the memo, the meeting is structured to connect all the parts: the statement of purpose, background, recommendation, and ratio-nale.

A typical meeting.

The typical P&G creative review meeting will start with the brand manager giving a statement explaining what the meeting is to attempt to accomplish. This is followed by a review of the creative objective and strategy—delivered by the brand manager or the assistant brand manager. The advertising agency account executive, the brand manager's counterpart, is then expected to describe the advertising development process that provides the bridge between the strategy and the advertising that is about to be presented.

The creative director or the copywriter, or both, then present the advertising. They do so with the vigor and enthusiasm that would be expected to accompany some of the most exciting advertising that has ever been created.

Then silence. The assistant brand manager, brand manager, and the marketing manager (the brand manager's boss) are all making notes.

The assistant brand manager responds first. His first remarks have to do with whether or not the material executed the advertising strategy for the brand—not whether he "likes it" or not. Other observations follow, usually related to how well the advertising conforms to the dos and don'ts that were learned in P&G's Copy College—the training program brand management people receive to learn how to evaluate advertising. The agency is allowed to respond, to explain how the advertising executes the advertising strategy for the brand.

The brand manager responds next, agreeing or disagreeing with the assistant brand manager's assessment and adding some observations of her own. The agency responds.

The marketing manager then builds on the preceding assessments. Often, some related experience from other P&G advertising is brought to bear. Some subjective assessment might be offered under the heading "informed judgment." Agency management responds. If the marketing manager is the most senior P&G person in the room, he will deliver the final assessment of the advertising. Then the brand manager sums up the observations, conclusions, decisions, and next steps.

P&G people are trained to appreciate the special nature of the creative process, and throughout the meeting they are careful not to criticize the work in a heavy-handed way (as described in Lesson #74). Nevertheless, the underlying structure of the meeting is very objective and purposeful, and it *does* keep the focus on the objectives, strategy, and the ultimate purpose of the advertising.

Basic principles of a P&G meeting.

Many meetings in corporate America are poorly planned and poorly conducted. It has been estimated that meetings in this country function at about thirty percent of maximum efficiency and effectiveness. Whether or not you run your meetings like a P&G meeting, some of the basic principles of the P&G meeting have universal application:

- Decide ahead of time what you hope to accomplish.
- Decide who should be at the meeting, and for what purpose.
- Prepare an agenda; send it out in advance of the meeting.
- Invite comments or revisions to the agenda prior to the meeting.
- Open the meeting with a review of the agenda, the meeting's objectives, and the pertinent background.

- Keep the meeting focused.
- Facilitate appropriate participation from all attendees.
- Establish next steps: who, what, how, and when.

By using a tight agenda, carefully spelling out the objectives at the beginning of the meeting, and giving someone the responsibility of keeping the meeting on track, you can probably get a lot more out of your meetings than you are now.

PASSING ON THE TRIBAL HISTORY

LESSON **39** ————————————————

The teaching hospital of packaged-goods marketing.

P&G is fanatical about training. Its future depends on it.

"The best training is on the job" is an axiom at P&G. P&G views the daily conduct of its business as a continuous learning and training experience. Supervisors are constantly providing feedback to their subordinates on an informal, ad hoc basis.

Every department also has a formal training program. In brand management, for example, there are required courses and seminars for all levels, ranging from a "Basic Advertising Principles" seminar for assistant brand managers to "Launching Successful Initiatives" for brand managers to "Category Market Leadership" and "Hard Calls" seminars for marketing directors. About ten percent of an assistant brand manager's time will be spent fulfilling the required training.

In addition, in every P&G office around the world, there are training catalogs of courses, workshops, and seminars in which employees can enroll—in consultation with their supervisor and linked to the development needs of the individual.

The "P&G College."

The P&G College is a relatively new program started by Ed Artzt in 1992. It had occurred to Artzt, and to some of his peers, that a lot of their thinking was grounded in their day-to-day exposure to an earlier generation of management—Richard R. Deupree, Neil McElroy, and Howard Morgens. Much of that exposure was in the form of anecdotes, including stories of *their* predecessors. And they talked about what was working, what wasn't working, and where the company was going. Artzt and his peers could *see* the values and principles held by this generation of management being applied to business decisions.

But the company had changed. It had grown bigger; so exposure to "the people on the eleventh floor" was more limited. More important, it had grown global. The next generation of management will likely have spent more of its time in Europe or the Far East or Latin America than in Cincinnati.

The purpose of the P&G College, therefore, is to pass on the experience and thinking of the senior managers of the company to the upcoming generation of managers. And to do it on a personal basis. The faculty of the P&G College is the CEO and the top management of the company.

New hires will spend several days at P&G College in their

first year. There are courses designed for first-time managers, then different levels of instruction as people get promoted. It's a rite of passage. Some four thousand employees
from every functional area and location go through the college every year.

LESSON **40** ————————————————————

The annual powwow.

*Every year the chiefs from all over the world come together
in the land of their ancestors.*

Every year, during the first week of November, the company holds a series of meetings in Cincinnati. Every general
manager in the world participates as well as many of the
staff department heads of the subsidiary offices—about 275
managers in all. The purpose is to share experiences; to
trade success stories; to inform others about initiatives, results, and key issues; and to reconnect to company goals
and strategies. One P&G manager described it as "taking
communion."

The week culminates in an event held at the Coliseum in
downtown Cincinnati. Of course, the CEO and COO have
their say; then senior managers from around the world add
the global perspective. Almost all of the Cincinnati P&G employees attend the event, and thousands of others in forty-
four locations around the world view it live via satellite.

CHAPTER

3

MANAGING FOR SUCCESS

A company's culture can give management a strong hand or a weak one, but it is the deck that the company's leadership deals from. Culture is bigger than management. The culture does not change with each new change of management, and if an incoming management team doesn't like what it sees, it cannot simply change the company's culture by proclamation. Ed Harness acknowledged the point this way: "We are built on sound principles and practices and are not dominated by a group of individuals. Though our greatest asset is our people, it is the consistency of principle and policy which gives us direction."

But management has a very important role in nurturing the culture. It must be a cheerleader for the culture. It must sustain and reinforce the culture that has worked for the organization. Homegrown management, such as P&G's, contributes to the perpetuation of a culture.

Management must also adapt the culture—or begin to modify it—to meet changing market conditions. That can be difficult if the cultural roots are deep.

A fundamental conclusion of *Built to Last* is that success-

ful, visionary companies are companies that have the ability
to adapt to changes in the marketplace while still maintaining their core values. These are companies that "preserve
the core and stimulate progress." P&G has demonstrated its
ability to do just that.

The first eight "lessons" in this chapter are about management actions that "preserve the core" and perpetuate the
culture in the way it interacts with the people of the organization. The last three lessons demonstrate management's
actions that "stimulate progress."

PRESERVE THE CORE

LESSON **41** ————————————————

Find the principle.

*Many business decisions have effects that go beyond beating
the competition or making a profit. It often comes down to
the hard choice between what's right for the long term
versus the short term. If decisions are inconsistent with
principles, the principles will ultimately be undermined.*

Management is importantly a moral undertaking.
—**John Smale, former P&G CEO**

Ed Harness defined the art of finding the principle:
"Making the hard decision, consistent with principle, usually involves two things—hard thinking by a disciplined
mind and short-term sacrifice on the part of the company."

In the late 1960s a controversy arose over detergents containing phosphates, which reportedly contributed to a major pollution problem centered mainly in Canada and the states of the Great Lakes basin. The quality of Great Lakes water was deteriorating, primarily as a result of improperly treated sewage and the runoff of agricultural wastes and fertilizers. Phosphates were identified by an international commission as one of the problems. Phosphates were a very visible target that the public could relate to. Housewives could do something about their own contribution to pollution by cutting back their use of detergents containing phosphates and pressing their local governments to ban them.

Some detergent manufacturers tried to capitalize on the public's anxiety by introducing nonphosphate brands. These products didn't do much to get clothes clean, however. Worse, they used highly alkaline and corrosive ingredients and could be harmful.

P&G refused to pander to the consumer hysteria with inferior or harmful products, and when the states of New York and Indiana, and several cities, including Chicago, passed laws banning detergent brands that contained phosphates, P&G withdrew their phosphate brands from those markets.

Throughout the controversy, P&G had argued that phosphate detergents were a negligible cause of pollution. Eventually, as proper sewage treatment was expanded and the quality of the Great Lakes water improved, the commission relented, concluding that detergents contributed only two percent of all the phosphorus in the Great Lakes. The P&G brands were then reintroduced.

P&G lost some sales. And its management took a lot of heat at the time. But the company stood by its principles of concern for the consumer, product quality, and Doing the Right Thing.

LESSON **42** ————————————————

Honor your people.

As the culture is important to the company, so are its people. After all, without people there can be no culture.

P&G's four-page declaration of purpose, core values, and principles has this statement at the top of the Core Values page: "P&G IS ITS PEOPLE AND THE CORE VALUES BY WHICH THEY LIVE." It's a mantra with P&G management. At every opportunity—in speeches, corporate statements, annual reports, even some news releases—P&G extols the quality, commitment, leadership, innovation, perseverance, creative thinking, courage, dedication, hard work, performance, and energy of its people. Part of the mantra is an oft-quoted remark made in 1947 by P&G president Richard Deupree: "If you leave us our money, our buildings, and our brands, but take away our people, the company will fail. But if you take away our money, our buildings, and our brands, but leave us all our people, we can rebuild the whole thing in a decade."

Pioneering enlightened employee relations.

P&G has a rich history of improving the worker's lot. In the 1880s it pioneered the five-day workweek and, to the amazement of many in American industry, a profit-sharing plan. To be sure, there was an element of enlightened self-interest behind this on the part of management. It was betting that these employee benefits would improve worker efficiency, thus offsetting the costs of the improved benefits. But at least the company's management at the time was attuned to employee motivation and interested in emphasizing the "inseparability of interests" of the firm and its workers.

The fact that P&G employees and retirees own about twenty-five percent of the company's stock is more than simply symbolic of the inseparability of the interests of the firm and its workers. It provides a very real incentive for employees to care about the health of the company. And the company recently took the initiative to encourage even more stock ownership by employees. While many companies have stock-option programs for top management, P&G is offering a stock option program for *all* employees. Every employee as of May 15, 1998, has the option to purchase one hundred shares of P&G stock, at the price of the stock on that date, anytime within the following ten-year period. This is not an insignificant gesture; if the company achieves its goals, the value of that option grant could be a billion dollars.

Caring for people.

P&G's concern for its people is manifested in other ways. Former P&Ger Tim Benton, for example, had a serious injury that put him on crutches for eighteen months and required specialized surgery in Atlanta and extensive rehabilitation. He said, "My coworkers and the company were very supportive of that. . . . Do I think the company cared about Tim Benton? I think they did. The actions they took proved that."

One of the most poignant personal stories was related by Kathleen Dillon Carroll, a former brand manager. Kathleen's family included her mother and three adolescent sisters who lived with her mother in Sherburne, New York. She said that when her mother became terminally ill, "they bent over backwards to make it work so I could be there for my mother and my sisters. They made it incredibly unstressful. P&G has a plant in Norwich, which is twelve miles from where my mother and sisters lived. They had a plane going back and forth between Cincinnati and Norwich, and they told me 'If there's an empty seat, you're in it.' John Pepper knew about it and supported it. And they promoted me in the middle of it! That meant even more to my mother than to me at the time—she was relieved to know that I wasn't sacrificing my career to be with her. I was not working at all in the last month, and they still paid me. They made a highly stressful situation much less so. To me that's ethics. It says 'we have values that guide us.' I will always think it's a phenomenal place."

LESSON **43** ————————————————————

Recruit the best people.

The best recruits make the best employees.

At Procter & Gamble, the ability to recruit effectively is a matter of survival because the company has a strict policy of promoting from within. It knows that the next generation of management will be developed from the ranks of today's rookies.

P&G works hard at recruiting. Strong relationships are developed with college placement offices and some faculty. Résumés are scanned for promising candidates, including those students who have not signed up for interviews. Top executives give talks at colleges. Line executives at all levels are involved in the recruiting and interviewing process.

P&G has developed tests that evaluate an applicant's aptitude for leadership and problem solving. The tests have been validated by the high test scores of successful P&G executives. The interviewing process is purposeful and behavior based. A candidate's past experience and accomplishments are examined for evidence of strong capabilities of leadership, problem solving, priority setting, initiative, follow-through, and ability to work with others. Top management is debriefed on recruiting results, and methods are constantly evaluated for possible improvement.

Companies that replenish their ranks from outside the company don't have to depend on entry-level recruiting to supply their management needs. Some get lax about the process—thus perpetuating a "revolving door" at the middle- and upper-management levels.

LESSON 44 ────────────────

Be a good coach.

A boss tells you what to do; a coach helps you learn as you do it.

▬▬▬▬▬▬▬▬▬▬▬▬▬▬▬▬▬▬▬

P&G is very focused on developing its people, and those with supervisory responsibilities are encouraged to treat every interaction with subordinates as a coaching opportunity.

Effective performance as a manager at P&G means two things: building the business and building the organization. Building the organization, in turn, is defined as taking responsibility for developing one's own capabilities as well as those of subordinates. Both the boss and the subordinate have a mutual interest in the subordinate's development, and the role of the boss is to facilitate that development.

The vehicle for this process, used around the world, is the Work and Development Planning System. An employee's so-called W&DP is linked to the OGSM (Objectives, Goals, Strategies, and Measures) of his or her department, and the department's OGSM is linked to the OGSM of the region and of the company as a whole.

The W&DP has four key components:

- the previous year's plan versus the results
- areas for further growth and development
- near-term and long-term career interests
- a development and training plan for the year ahead

The W&DPs are reviewed annually and updated regularly during the year when appropriate to reflect progress and changing priorities. The supervisor administering the program for the subordinate gathers feedback from internal and external sources who have firsthand experience in dealing with the person being reviewed. The emphasis, as suggested by the name of the program, is on development rather than evaluation. (The person being W&DP'd might perceive it somewhat differently, however, since it is also the basis for promotion and salary review!)

In addition to the formal review and updates of the W&DPs, supervisors are encouraged to supplement the program with informal, ongoing coaching. In a recent internal message, CEO John Pepper offered these tips:

- Treat *every* interaction with people who work for you as a coaching opportunity.
- Instruct on the principles, not just the details, of the issue at hand.
- Talk openly about mistakes and serve as a "safety net."
- Point out other individuals in the company who might be a resource for advice or a good model of a skill to be worked on.
- Ask your supervisor how you could be a better coach.

LESSON **45** ————————————————————

Make everyone a leader.

Push responsibility and decision making down into the organization.

> We must strive to avoid having employees feel that they are overmanaged.
>
> **—John Smale, former P&G CEO**

P&G's success in empowering employees to take an active leadership role in its plants is a good example. In his book *What America Does Right,* Robert Waterman describes P&G as a pioneer in pushing leadership, responsibility, and decision making down to the plant floor.

Dave Swanson was the principal architect of the organizational design of the system. Swanson joined P&G in the early 1950s after earning a master's degree in chemical engineering. While at MIT he had been intrigued and inspired by a professor at the Sloan School of Business, Douglas McGregor, who attacked the theory of command-and-control management and espoused a theory that would empower and enable each individual to make his or her maximum contribution to the business.

About eight years after Swanson joined the company, he had an opportunity to experiment with this theory when he participated in the design of a new detergent plant in Augusta, Georgia. He enlisted McGregor's help.

Processes were put in place to make communications and control flow up, down, and sideways in a very easy, uninhibited way. They emphasized knowledge of the business and learning new skills for all employees of the plant. The objective was to push the Augusta plant to be as unstructured as possible. "We were trying to take away the rule book and substitute principle for mandate. . . . We wanted people to reach for responsibility," Swanson said.

They did. Plant productivity went up thirty percent, and the system was expanded to other P&G plants.

Waterman's description of the P&G plant in Lima, Ohio, is a good example of how the system has evolved. Management focuses on what needs to be done. For example, increase the speed of getting a new product to market, improve the service to Wal-Mart, manage diversity more proactively. *How* it gets done is left up to the "technicians," as the line employees are called, and the teams assigned to the tasks. If they don't understand the goals of management, or if they disagree with them, they are encouraged to say so. That's important. Sometimes the employees who are closest to the situation have a perspective that management has not appreciated. The goals can be changed. And if management does not change the goals, it does so in a way that the employees can understand and take "ownership" of.

The compensation structure is another part of the system that encourages employees to take responsibility for the business. It is called a skill-based pay system. People get paid for what they know and what they are able to accomplish—rather than for seniority or movement up the traditional hierarchy. And it's all salary. No special bonuses tied to outstanding individual performance. There are other forms of recognition, but compensation is tied to fundamental qualifications and performance capabilities.

There are five levels of compensation, tied to "Q-blocks," or qualification blocks. To move to the next Q-block level, the technician must be able to demonstrate to his or her fellow team members a specified level of knowledge of the manufacturing processes and plant systems. The team—consisting of the individual who has worked most closely with the candidate, another individual already qualified, the manager of that process department, other already qualified individuals of the candidate's choosing, *and* the candidate himself or herself—decides whether or not the candidate is qualified to move to the next level.

One engineer who had been a manager in operations for a big steel company before he joined the Lima plant said that at the steel plant tight job descriptions and a rule book dictated how work got done. But at Lima, it's principles, not rules, that guide the process. That can make it more frustrating at times. It also makes it more challenging, interesting . . . and human.

Penetrate the business.

Encouraging employees to take on responsibility and leadership functions does not imply that managers should disengage from the business. P&G managers spend a high proportion of their time in the "engine room" of the business. They call it "penetrating the business." They are involved managers.

Ed Harness emphasized "management by penetration" as an important P&G trait: "At every level, we expect our managers to penetrate the operations of those reporting to them." Top managers of the company routinely visit R&D and production facilities and go out into the marketplace on store checks or attend consumer focus groups. One senior manager said he tried to spend at least two hours a month listening in on incoming phone calls from the 800 number that is printed on the brands' packages. The senior managers might not know as much about a particular brand as that brand's brand manager, but they know enough to ask some *very* penetrating questions.

The P&G memo helps make it work. Routine reports, such as sales and share analyses or market research reports, are passed up the line to keep management plugged into the business. In addition to information reports, recommendations are also passed on up the line—beyond the level at which the decision is made—for the purpose of keeping top management informed. Memos, with their distilled cover memos, make it easy for top management to consume huge quantities of information.

The net effect of all this "penetration" of the business is twofold. First, it taps the cumulative experience of the managers all the way up the line. Even if a decision is made at a lower level, a more senior manager is not hesitant to question the rationale if the decision is important enough. Second, it assures that decisions will be made for rational, strategic reasons. A recommendation to air a new advertising campaign will not be approved because it "feels right" to the brand manager. The rationale will be there and the decision will be defendable.

LESSON **47**

Reward real performance, not just results.

Results are very important, but results are not the only *measure of performance.*

P&G managers are evaluated on two criteria: growing the business and growing the people. Realistic and specific goals are established for each individual. Advancement is based primarily on measurable results compared against these goals. However, circumstances beyond an individual's control are taken into account.

Goals are adjusted to a realistic time frame. If it takes three years to see meaningful results, the measurements are adjusted accordingly. Extenuating circumstances and outside factors beyond an employee's control are taken into account. If targeted results are not achieved, the employee is not necessarily penalized. Even if targeted results *are* met, the employee is judged to have underperformed if opportunities have been missed.

Other companies live by results only—no questions asked. A recent *New York Times* article, for example, cited ConAgra's decentralized system, which generously rewards operating managers who perform based on strict annual financial criteria. Those who fall short get fired. ConAgra's frozen food division had four managers in five years. The company's culture gives almost total autonomy to its managers and encourages short-term, opportunistic measures and a "pounce-at-any-opportunity" approach to daily operations of its units. Unlike in the P&G culture, there's no incentive to consider long-term effects of any actions, to seek the involvement and understanding of top management, to cooperate with other divisions, or to Do the Right Thing.

LESSON 48 ─────────────────

Keep succession planning on a short leash.

Maintain and continuously review an inventory of top people considered to be replacement candidates for management positions. Stay flexible. It is not necessary to have a formal, long-term succession.

The performance and career development of its people is a subject of constant discussion among P&G managers. Managers visiting manufacturing plants or subsidiary offices are reputed to ask first about the people, then about the business. And at the most senior level of the corporation, the executive committee, including the CEO and thirty or so top managers in the company, meets every week to review personnel and business issues. The company works hard to make sure it always has an ample inventory of people who are ready to move up. It must if promotion from within is to succeed.

While P&G looks for the most capable people in its organization to fill vacant positions, it also tries to place people in work situations where the development of the individual will be greatest. The company often asks its people to make moves that would not necessarily be ones they themselves would select—or want. Ed Artzt has said, "We often toss good guys into snake pits. What is key is to let the managers know that the moves are in their best interest. People have to be challenged and grow up the hard way. Accepting tough assignments requires that the people have faith and trust in the company. . . . We are reluctant to make promises. We don't want to make promises we can't keep. Also, we like to keep our options open. We might have to put a person in a lesser position than we had originally intended. For a person to accept this, there has to be faith in the company and in the superior. There also has to be a payoff eventually."

STIMULATE PROGRESS

LESSON **49** _____

Organize to nurture new ideas.

New ideas that don't have immediate obvious potential are often fragile and can easily be orphaned in a big organization. New ideas need champions—individuals or small rogue groups that can operate within the larger organization to create them and bring them to life. P&G has recognized the need to encourage champions of new ideas that are more than incremental innovations. P&G needs major new brands.

P&G wants to add $35 billion in sales over the next ten years. That's double its current volume. Incremental innovation and growth of existing brands in mature markets isn't going to do it. Global expansion of brands in underdeveloped markets will help, but that alone can't possibly accomplish the goal. The company must develop major new brands—billion-dollar brands.

The Innovation Leadership Team.

To help address this problem, the company instituted a program a few years ago called the Innovation Leadership Team (ILT) program. The ILT includes the CEO, the head of R&D, and five other top executives. The ILT provides seed funding for ad hoc teams within the organization that want to pursue a product idea or technology. But, typical of P&G, the ideas must be clearly envisioned. The proposals are not going to fly on the basis of their champions' passion alone. The teams who receive "grants" must have a game plan for defining the ideas and market potential, and a plan for testing their viability. The ILT meets six to eight times a year to parcel out $25 million or so to nurture these new ideas through the early phases of development—and to review the thirty-odd previously approved projects at specific checkpoints along the way.

The business sector new-ventures group.

To complement the ILT program, a new-ventures group was created within each business sector. When an idea developed by one of the new-ventures groups is ready to be brought to market, it is assigned to a brand group and folded into the mainstream organization of the business sector. At least five projects have been developed by the new-ventures groups and handed off to the business sector, including Febreze, a product that removes odors from fabrics and carpets, and Dryel, a product that dry-cleans clothes in the home dryer.

However, the business sector new-ventures groups are limited by the experience and resources of the particular business sector. They cannot be expected to identify and evaluate unmet consumer needs that do not fit neatly into their categories of business. Therefore the *corporate* new-ventures group was established.

The corporate new-ventures group.

The corporate new-ventures (CNV) group includes cross-divisional members from R&D, brand management, research, finance, and product supply and support. The group reports directly to P&G's president and has access to the technologies and resources of all of the business sectors.

Open communications among the team members, with a lot of sideways thinking and cross-fertilization of the disciplines, is essential. The CNV group's office space uses an open floor plan with no office doors. The CNV team members have acquired couches from the basement "giveaway" area and created a lounge of sorts with coffeemakers, soft drinks, and doughnuts readily available. They talk and share ideas with one another during the morning break and encourage "guests" from within the company to join the informal interchanges.

This is not to suggest that the group's approach is ad hoc or informal. It is very much in the P&G style. Their goal is to make the process of innovation as scientific and efficient as possible. They systematically examine the knowledge and technology that is already inside the company. They also explore trends in consumer demographics, technology, society, and industry and rely heavily on outside consultants to understand how various trend areas can create new markets. They reject the "Eureka!" or "stuff happens" models of innovation. Rather, they liken P&G and its vast resources to a gold mine, where CNV members are miners whose job it is to dig through tons of information ore to find a few usable nuggets.

P&G is confident that CNV is the right mechanism to help the company revitalize its historic capability of new category innovation. The recently announced ThermaCare HeatWraps is a good example of just such a new category innovation. ThermaCare HeatWraps—in test market in Eau Claire, Wisconsin, and Midland, Texas—are wearable, therapeutic wraps designed to help relieve muscle and joint pain. Nothing quite like them has existed before.

LESSON **50** ————————————————

Don't think outside the box. Change the box.

Thinking outside the box implies thinking or doing things outside of the established paradigm. If the established paradigm isn't working anymore, change it.

You've got to envision the risk in staying where you are. If we don't change, we are going to decline. And any decline in an institution is a threat to its survival.

—Ed Artzt, former P&G CEO

It is what you learn after you know it all that counts.

—John Wooden, former UCLA basketball coach

John Wooden is arguably the all-time greatest coach in college basketball history. Sure he had great players. But so did a lot of other coaches. The difference was that most coaches have one way of doing things, and they make the players fit into the coaches' style. The players fit into the coaches' boxes. Wooden would completely change the way the game was played every time he had a new set of players. He would assess his players' strengths and his competitors' vulnerabilities and play the game that worked to his best advantage. He kept changing the box.

P&G is criticized by many of its detractors, and even by a few admirers, as being so structured and rigid in its beliefs and routines that it is incapable of changing its way of thinking—of thinking "outside the box." Hence, they say, P&G is unable to react to changes in market conditions or to generate new and creative approaches to problems and opportunities. While it is true that P&G is slow to depart from beliefs and processes that have worked over time, P&G is an astute observer of the world around it. If the old ways aren't working, the company steps back, reevaluates how it is looking at the world, and when necessary, it changes the box.

Ex-P&Ger Chris Bachelder put it this way: "P&G knows that 'the box' has value. It applies time-tested principles. It provides the organization with an experience base and thought structure that enable them to work together efficiently. As the experience base and market conditions change, P&G will change the box with input from a lot of people and will let everyone know about the new box."

P&G has changed the box in some very significant ways.

Converting the retailer from an adversary to an ally.

With dominant brands in so many major grocery categories, P&G always enjoyed tremendous clout with the retail trade. P&G sales representatives, armed with consumer product-preference test results, share data, and test results from other markets, would virtually dictate what products the retailer should stock and how much shelf space would be allocated to P&G brands. When a discount, or "trade allowance," was offered on a P&G product, the sales rep would "suggest" how many cases of product the retailer should order, at what special price it should be featured in the retailer's advertising, and how it should be displayed in the stores.

Many retailers didn't mind at all. The retailer needed to run reduced-price promotions on the biggest brands in order to attract the most shoppers. And because P&G has such big, popular brands, the P&G reps had little trouble getting lower-price features and bigger product displays than their competitors. But the sales reps inevitably pushed until they *did* meet some resistance. In fact, it was a rite of passage for all new salespeople to be thrown out of a store for the first time. If you never got thrown out of a store, you weren't pushing hard enough.

Then the retail world changed. Retail industry mergers gave the big chains more clout. UPC bar codes and electronic checkout scanners gave the retailer instant information on what was selling and what was not, and the information the sales representative presented was less relevant and more dated. Supermerchants such as Wal-Mart began telling the manufacturers how they wanted to run their own business, rather than the other way around. Membership warehouse clubs such as Costco and Pace were moving huge amounts of volume at "everyday low prices." They didn't stock all brands—just the brands that offered the best price day in and day out.

P&G responded to this changed world.

It reorganized its sales organization. Instead of covering each account with sales organizations from five product divisions in three sales layers, the company organized the sales force into account teams. Each major retailer now has a P&G team dedicated to it that represents not only all five divisions but also the functions of marketing, logistics, finance, and technology. Many of these teams, called customer business development teams, live in the headquarter city of the accounts and work in partnership with their counterparts in the account organization. P&G pioneered an automated continuous-product-replenishment system with Wal-Mart that significantly reduced customer inventories and replenished retail outlets directly from the factory as products moved out through the checkout counter. Intimidation and bullying tactics, which can be effective in an adversarial relationship, are no longer appropriate. The goal now is to build the business for both organizations. The replenishment system was adapted to other customers, and competitors followed suit.

The elimination of trade promotions.

Then, to bring costs down and match the big retailers' pricing strategies, P&G shocked the packaged-goods industry in late 1991 by announcing an EDLP (everyday low price) policy and the virtual elimination of its trade promotion. The company was able to fund the price reductions with the savings from the discontinued promotions and from manufacturing efficiencies. By eliminating the periodic surges and cutbacks in production caused by the promotions, P&G estimated it boosted production efficiency from fifty-five percent to eighty percent.

From proliferation to simplification.

P&G has always been a prolific marketer of different brands within a category—and of different flavors, sizes, and packaging versions of its bigger brands. Not long ago, there were fifty-two versions of Crest toothpaste alone. P&G's competitors also marketed a lot of sizes and shapes of their brands. That's just the way the game was played.

P&G was particularly good at the game. It was another point of competitive advantage for P&G. When P&G came out with a new brand or a line extension (for example, a new size, form, flavor), retailers were less inclined to resist the product than they might have been with other manufacturers; they needed P&G brands and knew that P&G promoted them heavily to the consumer. Then P&G had an army of sales people and detailers patrolling the grocery and drugstore aisles to make sure those varieties resulted in extra shelf space for its brands.

In the early 1990s, the proliferation was getting out of hand. By 1996, there were about 31,000 SKUs (stock-keeping units, or different items) in the average U.S. grocery store, an increase of roughly thirty-five percent from five years earlier. So stores were crammed with SKUs that weren't moving. According to research conducted by Kurt Salmon Associates, almost a quarter of the products in a typical supermarket were selling fewer than one unit a month. Most of the sales were generated by relatively few products. For example, according to Paine Webber analyst Andrew Shore, just eight percent of all personal-care and household products account for about eighty-five percent of sales.

This trend had not gone unnoticed by the big retailers. Strengthened by their newfound leverage with the manufacturers, the retailers began to drop slow-selling brands and varieties of brands. Real-time automation enabled the retailer to seize control of his business.

The proliferation strategy no longer gave a competitive advantage to P&G. Besides, it was inefficient to produce low-volume items. It was estimated to have added three to five percent to the cost of goods.

So P&G changed the box. In 1993 P&G announced that it was reducing the number of SKUs and eliminating some of its low-volume brands altogether. The company was changing the rules of the game—even though those rules had favored it more than most of its competitors. The industry was shocked.

The company cut the colors, flavors, shapes, and sizes of its hundred U.S. brands by fifteen to twenty-five percent. In hair care alone, P&G slashed the number of variations by almost a third. It lost some sales volume at first, as inventories of the discontinued items were not replenished. But despite the worst fears of the traditionalist thinkers, overall sales did not go down. They went up. Other packaged-goods marketers have fallen in line; P&G has changed the box for the industry.

Rethinking the organization.

But P&G's problems ran deep. The company's growth in the 1980s was falling behind its historical trend line. The elimination of trade promotion and the simplification strategies were, in Ed Artzt's words, "just attacking the symptoms of a broader problem." Costs were still too high. P&G's best consumers in the U.S. paid $725 a year more for P&G brands than they would have for private label or low-priced brands. Sales and market share of most P&G brands lacked vitality, and consumers seemed to be sending the message that the premium price of P&G brands was a lot of money for a middle-class American family. In addition, the company was not outdoing its major competitors, who were getting leaner and faster to market. In the wake of the takeover frenzy of the late 1980s, it was not incomprehensible that P&G could become a takeover target. The company had to improve its performance.

A program called Strengthening Global Effectiveness was put into place. A group of eleven teams examined every part of the company. The teams delivered more than 150 action recommendations to eliminate duplication, streamline work processes, and drive out costs that didn't translate directly to value for the consumer.

A wrenching restructuring was launched. Thirty of P&G's 147 plants around the world were closed. The workforce was reduced by twelve percent, eliminating thirteen thousand jobs and resulting in a $1.5 billion charge against fiscal 1992–93 earnings. Layers of management were reduced. Work processes were simplified. As a result, list prices of nearly all of its U.S. brands were reduced by twelve to twenty-four percent. Growth and profitability followed, both domestically and outside the U.S.

The ability of the company to overhaul its work processes and reengineer itself is remarkable. Successful companies with strong cultures and ingrained habits can be very resistant to change. But P&G's disciplined, long-term, strategic approach, and its determination to do what is necessary to win in the marketplace, inevitably led to the necessary decisions. Downsizing was handled largely through attrition, the consumer received enhanced product value, the stockholder was rewarded with improved revenue and profitability, and the stability of the company was reestablished.

LESSON **51** _____

Different styles for different times.

Companies have different needs at different times. Some managers are better suited to different tasks than others.

The late 1970s and the 1980s were not particularly robust years for P&G in terms of net income growth, return on capital, and growth of stock price. There were some short-term reasons for this that were not directly related to the basic health of the business. The company was hit with the Rely tampons withdrawal, sank a lot of capital into building disposable-diaper plants, and was digesting acquisitions such as Richardson-Vicks and Norwich Eaton Pharmaceuticals. However, P&G's basic business was not picking up the slack. The future did not look great.

When it came time to anoint a successor to CEO John Smale in 1990, tradition suggested that John Pepper would be the choice. As president, Pepper was next in line for the job and was highly qualified. He had risen through the brand management ranks on a very fast track. He was well-respected by his peers and well-liked by the rank and file.

A lot of people were startled when it was announced that Ed Artzt would be the next CEO. Pepper was made head of P&G International, taking over the position held by Artzt. Some speculated that Smale and the board decided that Pepper, then only fifty-one, had plenty of time for his turn at the helm and needed more seasoning in the emerging global marketplace.

Or perhaps they chose Artzt because he was the right manager for the time. By his own definition, Artzt was a "wrecking crew." "If it doesn't work right," he said, "I break it down and build it up again." Not exactly a typical P&G style of management.

Artzt had a history of creating radical change within the company. He had "fixed" the paper division in the mid sixties following several failed attempts to grow this acquisition. He was then assigned the task of turning around the food products division, then, in 1970, the coffee division. He cracked heads. Blame was assigned and people were reassigned. The moniker Prince of Darkness was coined and stuck throughout the rest of his career. He was decisive, autocratic, and anything but a consensus builder. He was thought to be overstepping his bounds by staff groups, but no one dared get in his way. He did what he was sent in to do—create radical change—even if the corporate culture got rattled in the process.

In 1972 he was named a director of P&G's board, and a few years later he was put in charge of the European operations. At the time, international assignments were not regarded as mainstream assignments leading to top management. But the company was beginning to see the long-term importance of the international marketplace, and it had problems in Europe; the business was stagnating, and European managers were reluctant to change. It needed a manager who could effect radical change.

Artzt reorganized the European operation. He created a matrix management structure under which managers share responsibility for categories of products, for regions as well as for their own countries. He consolidated operations and closed plants. He cut thirteen percent of the workforce in the U.K. He found young managers cast in his own image such as Durk Jager, whom *Fortune* magazine described as "always blunt and sometimes surly." Artzt was made president of P&G International in 1984 and can be credited with transforming the company into a truly transnational organization.

In 1990, with the company's domestic business in the doldrums, it didn't seem to be a time for business-as-usual at P&G. Artzt got the nod as CEO and spearheaded the restructuring of the company. He was not popular. Several senior executives resigned, and the morale of the rank and file was badly shaken.

It seems Artzt did overstep his bounds when he used P&G's clout and influence to access phone call records in order to track down an inside "informer" placing calls to a *Wall Street Journal* reporter. That was a breach of the company's code of conduct for which Artzt apologized and from which, some say, he never recovered.

Some close to P&G say that Artzt championed Durk Jager, who was then in charge of the U.S. operation, to succeed him. The board chose Pepper. Pepper is seen as a consensus builder and a healer. It was his time.

CHAPTER

4

THINK GLOBAL, ACT LOCAL—AND VICE VERSA

P&G has been an international marketer for more than half a century. Even before World War II P&G had foreign business in England, Canada, Cuba, the Philippines, and Indonesia. After the war, the business expanded dramatically. But it was still an opportunistic add-on to the U.S. business. P&G was still an American company in terms of its core business and in terms of its thinking.

Then the world began to change. Political tensions eased, trade barriers began to come down, more and more companies were demonstrating the efficiencies of internationally focused manufacturing and marketing. P&G's international business was growing at such a rate that, by the mid 1980s, it was becoming apparent that it could surpass the domestic business in about a decade. The international business was no longer just an add-on to the U.S. business.

At about that time, P&G stumbled in Japan and had to decide whether to write it off or to commit to a successful reentry. It was a watershed decision. Japan is the second-largest consumer market in the world. Without an established business in Japan, P&G would never be a truly global company. It decided to commit.

Developing the business on a global basis is now a strategic objective of the company. Strategies for developing and disseminating brands and technologies have been globalized—as has top management's perspective. The last two CEOs, John Pepper and Ed Artzt, were well groomed in the international business before their elevation to the top spot. Durk Jager, the president and COO, is Dutch and has spent most of his career in Europe and the Far East. Top management of the company under the COO level has been restructured. The heads of the four regions of the world have been moved up to the executive-vice-president level and report to Jager. The head of the domestic U.S. operation, Wolfgang Berndt, is only one of four EVPs. He was born in Czechoslovakia and spent most of his career in P&G's European subsidiaries. Three of the four EVPs began their careers in a foreign P&G subsidiary and spent the majority of their P&G careers outside the U.S.

The ability and willingness of the company to realign its management structure and to globalize its brands and technologies reflects a long-term, strategic approach to adapting to the global marketplace. But P&G's core values have not changed.

THINK GLOBAL

LESSON **52** ————————————————————

Capitalize on the opportunities of a shrinking world.

The world is becoming smaller and the demand for superior solutions for basic human needs is increasing.

Capitalism is becoming more acceptable around the world; markets are being opened to private industry. Trade barriers are coming down. Communication technologies are bringing diverse peoples together. People in underdeveloped countries know what life is like in the U.S. and the rest of the world. The standard of living in underdeveloped countries is improving. They wear Nike shoes, drink Coca-Cola, and they want the best products—products that are used in the more developed countries.

P&G is capitalizing on the opportunities to meet these universal needs with its products. People all over the world need cleaning products for their clothes, dishes, hair, bodies, and teeth. Bodily functions addressed by such products as diapers, sanitary napkins, and toilet tissue are the same the world over.

LESSON **53** ————————————————

Create global brands.

Seek opportunities to meet universal consumer needs with
universal brands.

Until the mid 1970s, P&G did not really think on a global basis. Most of their international business consisted of U.S. brands transplanted to other countries, or local brands created by P&G subsidiaries.

The company began to think about leveraging brands and technology on a transnational basis in the European marketplace in the late 1970s. This was a significant shift in thinking that was a precursor to true globalization about ten years later. To create global brands required a change in the way the company was managed across borders.

In Europe, as elsewhere in the world, P&G subsidiaries were all patterned after the U.S. organization in their manner of doing business. Each subsidiary was accountable for its own sales volume and profitability, and they had a considerable amount of discretion as to which products to market in their countries, and when. The autonomy of the subsidiaries was justified by the differences in consumer preferences and market conditions. For detergents, for example, there were country-to-country differences in water softness levels, types of washing machines used, legal restrictions related to ingredients, and consumer habits. As a result, P&G's Ariel detergent had nine different formulas throughout Europe. It was positioned diversely as a low-suds or a high-suds powder, for low- or high-temperature usage, depending on the country.

In the late 1970s, it was becoming apparent that the importance of some of the differences among countries had been exaggerated. After all, within the U.S., there were differences in washing machines, water softness, and consumer habits that were easily managed without requiring nine different formulations. It was also becoming apparent that the autonomy of the subsidiaries resulted in two problems.

First, the competition could "knock off" P&G's successes in some countries before P&G subsidiaries adapted them to other countries. Pampers diapers, for example, were introduced in Germany in 1973 but not launched in France until 1978, which was too late. Colgate had seen what was happening in Germany, launched a product named Calline with a package color, product positioning, and marketing strategy similar to those for Pampers, and captured the dominant share of the market.

Second, highly autonomous subsidiaries were inefficient. Duplication of R&D, product development, marketing, and administrative groups in each subsidiary resulted in an overhead expense in the subsidiaries that was fifty percent higher than in the U.S. By the mid 1970s, market growth had come to a standstill, cost pressures related to the oil crisis had increased, the competition had become more aggressive and was scoring some victories, and P&G's profit and sales growth had seriously eroded. Something had to be done.

The Europeanization of brands and a new management paradigm.

Wahib Zaki, the European R&D manager, devised a solution for the R&D organization in the late 1970s that provided the paradigm for the entire P&G operation in Europe and, ultimately, around the world. Zaki was determined to define a long-term European approach to product development. He decided to focus all the European R&D resources around key brands and develop pan-European products that would be superior to existing local products. The need for local adaptation would be minimal.

He did this by creating technical teams to work on products and technologies that had multiple-market potential. The members of the team in the Brussels European Technical Center would concentrate on the basic technologies ("putting the molecules together," as one R&D manager described it), while technicians at the subsidiaries took responsibility for testing and refining the products in the field. Lead countries were named for each of the key products, thereby giving more responsibility and ownership for the development process to the local subsidiaries and ensuring ongoing coordination and cooperation among them. It was clear that the local subsidiaries had to be fully involved and committed to the Europeanization effort.

The multinational management of P&G brands was patterned after the European technical teams. The key to making the so-called Euro Brand Teams work (versus an earlier failed attempt) was the involvement of the general managers of the subsidiaries. In addition to the traditional volume and profit responsibilities for their own countries, general managers were given regional responsibilities. Their charter was to coordinate the analysis of opportunities for the standardization of brands' product formulations and marketing activities and to coordinate activities across subsidiaries to eliminate needless management duplication. The general managers of all the subsidiaries were directly involved and were invited to one another's Euro Brand Team meetings. It was in the general managers' best interests to cooperate with one another's efforts.

This is, essentially, the same system that now ties the P&G subsidiaries together around the world.

LESSON **54** ─────────────────────

Japan: the global cornerstone.

Japan is the largest consumer market in the world outside the U.S. and arguably the toughest, most competitive, fastest-moving consumer market in the world.

> Compete with them in their own backyard, for you will eventually have to compete with them at home. . . . We need to be in business in Japan, and we cannot afford to be anything but successful there.
>
> **—Ed Artzt, former P&G CEO**

By the mid 1970s, P&G had a decent international business in many parts of the world. But its business had been opportunistic—essentially taking existing brands and marketing them wherever the company could make a profit. P&G was firmly entrenched in the European market, but there were vast areas of the world that it had not entered. The company's initial attempt in Japan was a wake-up call and a challenge to its ability to be truly competitive on a global scale. If P&G failed in Japan, it would be difficult for it to become a truly global company.

In the 1970s, P&G had entered Japan through a joint venture with a small Japanese detergent company. P&G was full of confidence, enthusiasm—and arrogance. After all, the companies behind McDonald's restaurants, Levi's jeans, and Marlboro cigarettes had all been successful in Japan doing things U.S. style. So P&G stormed into the Japanese market with its American products, American managers, American advertising, American sales methods, and American promotional strategies. Then it bought out its Japanese partners and took one hundred percent control.

It was a near disaster. P&G's Japanese competitors made excellent products geared for the Japanese consumer and were aggressive in defending their positions. Ten years later, P&G had lost over $200 million. It was facing defeat and had to decide whether or not to bail out. As a business decision, bailing out made a lot of sense. Obviously, P&G was only a short way up a long and steep learning curve.

P&G decided to fight because it concluded that winning in Japan was of strategic importance for two reasons. First, Japan is the second-largest consumer market in the world. Second, it was imperative that P&G be able to compete with Japanese marketers not only in Japan but in the rest of Asia and around the world.

The Japanese consumer is uncompromising in her demand for quality, value, and service. She has grown up in an environment where virtually every company manufactures products to a standard of zero defects, and she has come to expect that level of quality in every product she buys. (When Pampers diapers were being imported from the U.S., the Japanese consumer detected flaws at triple the complaint level P&G was experiencing in the U.S.) The Japanese woman is skeptical of aggressive, comparative product claims. She lives in a world of limited space. She is the paragon of efficiency in the management of her household. She rules the roost, controls the purse strings, and raises the kids. She is fastidious when it comes to personal hygiene. The Japanese change their babies' diapers twice as often as their American or European counterparts. The pattern is the same with their sanitary napkins. Women in Japan generally work before and after children are raised. Hardly any Japanese mothers work if they have children at home. Child rearing is the number one priority for the Japanese woman, and her relationship with her children is uniquely close.

If P&G was to become a truly global company, it would have to be a winner in Japan. The decision to pursue that goal had enormous implications for the future of the company and was a turning point in the company's thinking. The thinking was global; the execution was local. *How* P&G became a winner in Japan is described in the "Act Local" section of this chapter.

LESSON 55 ────────────────

The China strategy: 1.2 billion people can't be ignored.

There is enormous potential in underdeveloped markets as they become less restrictive and as the standard of living rises among their huge populations. The companies that get there first reap the biggest benefits long-term.

Once P&G decided to become a truly global company, it began to take a long-term, strategic approach to establishing strong competitive positions in the key countries of the world.

In some markets, such as India, Indonesia, Brazil, and Argentina, that means playing catch-up to its multinational rivals, which have worked those territories for fifty years.

P&G is prepared to invest and do what it takes to establish a leadership position. Being the market leader in China is a strategic objective for the company. The cost of getting there is a tactical matter.

China is the largest underdeveloped market in the world. It has twenty percent of the world's population. Its per capita gross domestic product is only one-tenth that of the U.S., but its GDP is growing at a rate of thirteen percent a year and consumer spending is rising faster there than in any developed country.

If people in China were to use certain packaged-goods products at anywhere near the rate that people use them in the developed countries, the potential growth for a company like P&G would be enormous. For example, disposable diapers are used in only about two percent of diaper changes in China, compared to about ninety-eight percent in the U.S. And the per capita consumption of toilet tissue is 5.4 rolls per year in China compared to 53.3 rolls per year in the U.S. The Chinese may never be such profligate users of toilet paper as we are in the U.S., but if they come anywhere close as their standard of living climbs, the retail market in China will be in the vicinity of $5 billion—five times what it is in the U.S.

P&G sales in China are about $1 billion. That's about $.70 per person, compared to $60 a person in the U.S. P&G's leadership in the hair care, laundry, and disposable diapers categories gives them a solid beachhead, but the company wants to establish leadership in the other fifteen or so categories in which it competes.

ACT GLOBAL

LESSON **56** ———————————————————

One company; one culture.

The P&G culture has been successfully exported around the globe. In the words of John Smale: "Procter & Gamble people all over the world share a common bond. In spite of cultural and individual differences, we speak the same language. When I meet with Procter & Gamble people—whether they are in sales in Boston, product development at the Ivorydale Technical Center, or the management committee in Rome—I feel I am talking to the same type of people. People I know. People I trust. Procter & Gamble people."

The cultures of many societies around the world are incompatible with P&G's culture and the "Procter Way" of conducting its business. Think of the P&G meeting as described in Lesson #38 in the context of some foreign countries' cultural norms. In some countries, neither business nor social meetings start on time. In others, meetings begin with a lot of conversation "around" the subject to let everyone participate before getting down to the issues and end with no definitive conclusions, next steps, and commitments. Some cultures are inclined to work toward consensus and avoid confrontation. Others are very hierarchical and autocratic and, unlike P&G's culture, don't demand initiative, commitment, and leadership from middle and lower levels.

How does P&G transplant such a strong corporate culture into a foreign country that has its own culture—especially when non-Americans from the local country make up the bulk of its staff? First, it starts out with seasoned management imported into the country, people who started their careers at P&G in the U.S. or elsewhere in the world and are steeped in the company's culture. These are internationalists, people who move from country to country. Then they recruit and hire nationals out of the country's colleges and universities who seem to have an affinity for the P&G culture. During the interview process, recruiters talk extensively about the Procter Way, and the applicants who are not comfortable with it are not hired. Those who are hired get extensive indoctrination and training.

The P&G culture in Czechoslovakia.

The culture can be learned. P&G's acquisition of the Rakona manufacturing facility in Czechoslovakia offers a good example of this process. The Eastern Europeans had grown up in a communist culture. The system had offered employees no incentive to do a good job. As the old saying goes, "We pretend to work; they pretend to pay us." If anything, people worked *around* the system and even tried to undermine it. But when people understand that the free enterprise system can work in their interest, they understand, in P&G terminology, "the inseparability of the interests of the company and its employees."

Rakona was the largest single maker of laundry and dish-washing detergents in Czechoslovakia. It was state-controlled, production was inefficient, and product quality was awful. P&G was exploring acquisition candidates and did a test production run to see if the Rakona plant could produce P&G's Ariel laundry detergent at anywhere near the quality of its German-made product. The employees of the facility, working hand-in-hand with P&G people, produced a laundry detergent that was indistinguishable from the German-made product—and did it six weeks ahead of schedule. The Czech management and workers had an incentive to perform. They wanted to impress the P&G people so that P&G would acquire the factory rather than one of the other companies that had come in to examine the operation. It seems that those companies were single-mindedly focused on how they could reduce the workforce and cut costs. In contrast, the P&G engineers who inspected the facility were focused first and foremost on how they could work with the current employees to produce better products. P&G bought the plant, the workers have incentives to produce, and the plant is churning out quality product for the Eastern European market.

The P&G culture in Japan.

The Japanese have also proven they can embrace the P&G corporate culture. In some ways, the Japanese culture is very compatible with a corporate culture such as P&G's. Country, company, and family are the three dominant social institutions in the life of the Japanese. They are unusually loyal to their employers, beyond anything we see in the U.S. Japanese graduates entering the marketplace don't just want a job; they want to make a lifelong commitment. Recruiting top-flight people from Japanese universities is extremely difficult for new foreign companies because of the history of failures and pullouts of foreign companies. When P&G made known its long-term commitment to succeed in Japan and as the quality of its products became known, P&G made a lot of recruiting headway. But what was particularly relevant to the young Japanese graduates was the

P&G policy of developing its people, promoting from within based on performance, and providing career opportunities. In a recent study among Japanese students, P&G was ranked among the top ten companies in Japan and was the only American company on that list.

LESSON **57** ————————————————

The multinational training model.

P&G's multinational training program internationalizes and homogenizes methodologies, processes, and practices and adapts them to different countries around the world.

Prior to 1980, P&G used the training model typical of many American corporations: employees were transferred from Cincinnati to the international subsidiaries where they managed the site and trained the local employees. In the early 1980s, as P&G was being transformed from an American company with some international sales to a truly global company, it initiated a new approach to multinational training.

P&G now has about a thousand expatriates from different countries working in locations outside their own countries. These managers help to internationalize and homogenize the P&G culture around the world as they move from country to country. An important part of the P&G multinational training model is the training of the incoming expatriates—training that includes understanding the local culture and its social and business environments as well as learning the language. In the view of a P&G international training and development manager, "As companies become more global, and employees spend more time working in other cultures, the line[s] between the cultures become less distinct."

Most of P&G's standard training curriculum is adopted worldwide. But, the local training staff adapts the courses and presents them locally. P&G believes that a successful training program cannot be run from the United States alone and that the best training is localized and run by managers from that country.

LESSON **58**

Principles are universal.

P&G lives by the same principles and the same code of business conduct around the world.

According to one incident from company lore, a shipment of Pampers top-sheet material, worth about a quarter of a million dollars, arrived at a country in West Africa. The customs inspector pretended that this material fell under a classification that forbade its import—but he was willing to release the shipment for a bribe of $5,000. The division manager refused. No discussion. The material remained blocked and the P&G operation had to shut down its plant for four months. The division manager could easily have justified the payment as a pittance relative to the cost of shutting down production. Some companies look at bribes as simply a part of the cost of doing business and necessary in order to compete in some parts of the world. Not P&G.

Ed Harness probably made the strongest statement about P&G's position on bribes and illegal contributions following the Watergate incident. One bit of fallout from the Watergate-related investigations was the revelation that some U.S. firms not only made illegal political contributions in the U.S. but also payoffs to foreign governments and officials of other countries. Harness had the confidence to say, "I want to assure you simply and flatly that this company has made no illegal political contributions to anyone in this or any other country, that this company makes no unethical political contributions anywhere in the world, that this company pays no bribes to anyone anywhere in the world, and that this company does not deal under the table with customers or suppliers here or abroad. That is the way this company has operated; that is the way we will continue operating."

LESSON **59**

Simplify and standardize.

Whenever possible apply existing packages, product formulas, or advertising campaigns to as many markets as possible, rather than reinvent every brand for every market. It saves money and time.

> Where there's no justification for differences, the brand is the same in every part of the world.
>
> **—Robert Wehling, P&G senior vice president, advertising**

Pampers, Pantene, Whisper, Pringles, and Oil of Olay are global megabrands whose products have more similarities than regional differences. Vidal Sassoon shampoos and conditioners contain a single fragrance worldwide, with variations only in amount—less in Japan, where subtle scents are preferred, more in Europe. Ariel detergent, a European megabrand, is sold throughout Central and Eastern Europe in the same package with fourteen languages printed on it.

Television commercials are similar from country to country, using local actresses and actors but the same basic format. A very successful campaign for Pringles used the same format—a rap-music theme and young people dancing around to the tag line, "Once you pop, you can't stop"—in the U.S. and in Germany. Often variations are produced for several countries in a single location, thus assuring comparability and saving money.

THINK LOCAL

LESSON **60**

Search and reapply.

Look for ideas that are successful elsewhere to adopt for the local market. "Search and reapply" is a key marketing tenet that the P&G subsidiaries apply with vigor.

According to a former regional manager of one of P&G's advertising agencies:

If you are a brand person in a marketplace, you are constantly looking for what's worked somewhere else. It's driven into their skulls. You don't do anything without seeing what else has been done.

The senior people are totally into the business. They don't just manage and make sure there's an exchange of information. *They* are personally knowledgeable about what is going on with other brands in the different countries and regions. The search and reapply culture comes down from the top and it works.

The P&G memo keeps everyone in the loop. Written reports are routinely circulated. And they are constantly meeting. Different levels of the organization as well as different functions. Product development people. Brand people. For information exchange as well as idea generation. They function like a company without borders.

When asked about the not-invented-here factor, he said, "They just won't abide it. It's a cultural thing. More than any company I've seen."

The search-and-reapply concept relates to products, packaging, marketing, advertising, promotion, and even manufacturing and distribution. A good idea usually has some common denominators that translate across borders.

P&G's recent success with Joy detergent in Japan is a good example. The highly concentrated version of this American dish-washing detergent was launched in Japan in 1996. It is based on a new technology developed specifically for Japan by P&G's scientists in Europe. The commercial was an adaptation of the documentary style "Show and Smell" campaign originally created for Daz detergent in Britain and subsequently adapted to Gain in the U.S. The leak-free cap that was developed in Japan for the brand is now being used on P&G products in the U.S. And the Joy product and marketing program that was so successful in Japan is now being adapted for the Philippines and is being considered for other Asian markets.

LESSON **61** _____

Understand the local consumer.

Basic consumer needs—such as the desire for a more
attractive complexion, or drier babies, or cavity-free
teeth—seldom vary. But the unique consumer perceptions
or characteristics of the local marketplace can dictate
different marketing strategies.

P&G learned the importance of understanding local consumer perceptions and market characteristics many years
ago. As P&G expanded internationally after World War II,
it did so by marketing U.S. products without giving much
consideration to local habits and tastes. In England, for example, it introduced a toothpaste with a wintergreen flavor.
Had the company done its homework, it would have learned
ahead of time that the idea of wintergreen as a flavor was
abhorrent to Britishers. Wintergreen was used there in lini-
ment, not in food or toothpaste.

Then the winter after P&G introduced Drene shampoo
in England, complaints began to roll in that the liquid crys-
tallized in the bottle. The company hadn't realized that the
temperature in many bathrooms in England was often
lower than the point at which the product would crystallize.

P&G must have forgotten this experience when it entered Japan years later. A fundamental reason for the initial
stumble in Japan was it did not understand the Japanese
consumer's perceptions and needs.

Cheer laundry detergent was P&G's first major entry in
the Japanese market, and it was a direct lift from the U.S.
The product had the unique advantage of getting clothes

clean in any washing temperature—hot, warm, or cold. But most Japanese women washed their clothes in cold tap water. The idea of washing in three different temperatures had no relevance to them. The product flopped. In fact, the practice of transplanting U.S. brands and marketing programs into the Japanese market—without adaptation to the local culture—was a major reason P&G nearly went out of business there.

ACT LOCAL

LESSON **62**

Adapt products to the local market.

Whenever possible, it is efficient to use a "standard" or existing formulation or size of a product in multiple markets. But often the impact of unique consumer perceptions or characteristics of the local marketplace more than offsets the cost-effectiveness of simplification and standardization. A good understanding of the consumer often dictates different products and different marketing strategies.

P&G committed itself to understanding the local consumer.

A key to successfully rebuilding the business in Japan was understanding the Japanese consumer. Once P&G

made that commitment, it approached the market very differently. The company brought Japanese nationals into its brand groups, hired a Japanese advertising agency, and blanketed the market with researchers in an effort to understand everything it could about the consumer: *in situ* research in the home, focus groups, shopper intercepts, concept tests, product tests. P&G listened and learned.

Resuscitating Cheer.

To resuscitate Cheer in Japan, P&G reintroduced the brand in a high-density formula in very compact packages that had a real space-saving benefit for the Japanese consumer. An appealing new lemon fragrance gave the brand a uniqueness it had lacked. P&G finally managed to establish Cheer in the Japanese market.

Later, P&G scientists invented a low-temperature bleach activator. This seemed to have promise for application to the Japanese cold-water market. P&G combined a new detergent formulation with a highly compact product and package in a new brand called Ariel, a name borrowed from its very successful brand in Europe. With Cheer and Ariel, P&G is now successfully established in the Japanese market.

Understanding the local consumer defined the high-potential target segment for Whisper.

P&G had an excellent product with which to enter the sanitary napkin market in Japan. Its Whisper sanitary napkin was preferred two to one in blind tests versus the established Japanese market leader. But P&G learned it had two problems to deal with. First, Japanese women were fastidious and circumspect about personal matters and not particularly receptive to giving up their familiar brand. Second, Whisper was relatively expensive to make and cost more than the leading local brands. Japanese women were not likely to switch to a more expensive newcomer to the market.

However, P&G learned that Japanese women in their late teens and twenties thought differently from the older consumer. They were more likely to try new products of this nature, more concerned about the problems that Whisper solved, and far less sensitive to price. P&G decided to focus its entire marketing effort on the younger age group.

The strategy was carried through in the advertising. The brand group and their advertising agency, the Dentsu organization in Japan, chose a well-known woman photographer who was a minor celebrity and an ideal role model for the emerging professional working women in Japan. Equally important was the *way* the spokesperson talked—reflecting the open and frank way young Japanese women talk to one another about personal matters. Her candid discussion of the product, and the concept that it felt "like wearing just-washed underwear," were symbolic of the desire of young Japanese women to achieve liberation in Japanese society. The results of P&G's doing its homework and responding to the differences within the culture paid off handsomely.

Japanese consumers wanted a different disposable diaper.

When P&G first introduced disposable diapers in Japan, the company used the American product. It was not a big hit. The American product was thicker—and more expensive—than it had to be. Besides, Asian babies are smaller than American babies. P&G redesigned a product that was smaller, three times thinner, less expensive, and packaged in a more compact way so that it was easier to store in the more limited space of the Japanese home and easier to travel with.

Different shampoo formulas for China.

In China, dandruff is a big problem that few Chinese shampoos solved. P&G entered the market with Head & Shoulders and followed with Rejoice (Pert in the U.S.) and Pantene, adding antidandruff formulas to each. P&G's shampoo-and-conditioner products in the Asia-Pacific region also use different levels of conditioners adjusted to the hair follicle thickness of Asians. The three shampoo brands together have earned over fifty percent of the market in the major cities of China.

Small-size packages in Peru.

Although P&G has had great success with compact detergents in many other markets, it does not market them in Peru. Most Peruvians can afford to buy only a small 250-gram package at any one time, and if P&G condensed the product, it would end up with a package of detergent the size of a tea bag. For the same reason, seventy percent of all shampoo is sold in single-use sachets in Peru.

A new way of sampling in China.

An understanding of the consumer and the idiosyncrasies of the local marketplace—plus a little ingenuity—can lead to some unique marketing approaches.

For example, product sampling has always been a very important marketing tool for P&G. Distributing samples in the U.S. is relatively straightforward. For some sampling programs, P&G's field sampling crews go house-to-house through selected neighborhoods hanging product samples in a plastic bag on door handles. For other programs, it's more cost-effective to target mailed samples to selected zip codes. In China, P&G came up with an even more reliable way to target and distribute product samples. Through the Communist Party! As reported in the September 15, 1995, *Asian Wall Street Journal:*

> Yuan Liuping is a foot soldier in the Procter & Gamble Company assault on China's consumer market.
>
> Ms. Yuan, a stooped, 72-year-old factory retiree who eyes strangers warily, leads a "neighborhood committee" in an alleyway maze that houses some 200 people. Here, she is the Chinese Communist Party's eyes, ears, and mouth.
>
> And an arm of Procter & Gamble's marketing machine. P&G recently hired her—and thousands of others—to pass out yellow-and-orange gift packets of Tide laundry detergent to neighbors. With Beijing's tentacles of political control aiding the most ambitious product launch in Chinese history, Tide colors now flutter from shop awnings from Beijing in the northeast to Chengdu in the southwest.

LESSON 63

Adapt the message to the market.

Creating products to fit consumers' needs is only part of the challenge. The messages must fit the way consumers hear—which means understanding the culture and tailoring the advertising so it will be heard and understood.

When Cheer was reintroduced, the Japanese brand group thought that the U.S. "Lemon Boy" puppet, the mainstay of P&G's U.S. Joy dish detergent commercials, would be a good advertising spokesman for the new Japanese Cheer product. But when they showed the U.S. Joy advertising to Japanese consumers, the Japanese judged the Lemon Boy character to be interesting but obnoxious and too aggressive. They described him as not positive, not helpful. The brand group decided to "Japanize" the puppet and make him more friendly, polite, but still enthusiastic. It worked.

In developing the advertising campaign for the introduction of Ariel detergent, the brand group found an effective way to compare the performance of the brand to that of the competition. In the Japanese culture, it is highly impolite and inappropriate to disparage others, and it is equally inappropriate for a company or a brand to disparage a competitor. P&G knew that. However, it had also learned that the Japanese consumer respects an objective presentation of factual information. The introductory Ariel advertising presented the performance of the product in a factual and objective manner and attributed the preference for Ariel to the judgment of Japanese homemakers who had tried both the Ariel product and the leading competitor.

The reintroduction of the thinner more compact Pampers had to overcome the carryover of the image problem left from the introduction of the original Pampers. P&G's research told the company that the extraordinarily doting Japanese mother thought of Pampers as a noncaring product. So P&G advertising created Pampers-chan, a talking diaper and fairy-tale character who talks to the baby and promises that the baby will be kept dry all over after a long night's sleep. The campaign helped Pampers lead an explosive expansion of the disposable-diapers market.

Camay is a toilet soap for facial and bath use. The bar and the wrapper look pretty much the same around the world. P&G has used many different advertising campaigns for Camay soap, but the scenario that has worked best in most countries takes place in a bathroom setting and is based on a strategy of "attractiveness to men." In France, the advertising is fairly direct, with an overt display of affection and a distinctively French touch of savoir faire. In the United Kingdom, the concept is conveyed with traditional British wit and understatement. An early attempt in the Japanese market included the good manners and politeness characteristic of the interaction between a man and a woman. Nevertheless, the advertising was immediately rejected by Japanese women. It is just plain bad manners for a husband to impose on his wife's privacy while she is bathing. No matter how polite he is about it. Consumers were offended by the breach of good manners and the overt chauvinism of the situation. Later, with the benefit of consumer insights, the Camay advertising capitalized on the appeal of Camay's European character and situated the commercial in a European setting with a European woman and western-style bath.

Adult incontinence is a delicate subject anywhere, and certainly no less so in Japan. There, the advertising for the adult disposable diaper, called Attento, takes advantage of the fact that in the Japanese culture storytellers are considered to be wise old men experienced and knowledgeable about life. The advertising features a well-known Japanese storyteller as the presenter for Attentos. He uses proverbs and humor to teach not only about life but about the functional advantages of Attentos.

LESSON **64** ———————————————————

Create a local image for the company.

In many countries, when an American company enters the marketplace, it is seen as the outsider, the foreigner, and sometimes perceived as the bully that takes business away from domestic companies and sends the money back to the United States. The local business community and suppliers don't know if the American company is committed to doing business there for the long term. And as an unknown, the company is not a respected organization that graduating university students aspire to work for, let alone build a career with. To be perceived as a local company, the subsidiary has to behave like a local company.

P&G works at expressing a commitment to the country whose marketplace it is entering. It conducts extensive interviews with the press, runs special corporate advertising, and meets with opinion leaders at universities and in the government.

P&G also promotes the company to the consumer. Japanese consumers are very company-conscious about the products they buy. They associate the quality, safety, and reliability of a product with the image of the company that makes it.

P&G was at a distinct disadvantage in relation to Kao, the huge Japanese packaged-goods company and P&G's principal domestic competitor. To learn what it was up against, P&G tested an identical product with two different panels of consumers—P&G was identified as its manufacturer to one panel, and Kao as the manufacturer to the other. The product identified as manufactured by Kao was significantly preferred. So now, in addition to corporate advertising, P&G devotes the last couple of seconds of its brand-advertising television commercials to associating the brand with the company. This approach has become an important part of the company's turnaround in Japan.

P&G also claims to be the first company in Japan to establish a toll-free telephone number for both consumers and the trade to call with any questions or comments. This, of course, helps P&G monitor consumer attitudes and immediately respond to any problems, but it also demonstrates the kind of corporate commitment to quality and service that the Japanese admire.

LESSON **65**

Work with suppliers and customers on their terms.

In the U.S. and Western Europe, P&G has taken the lead to find new ways to apply advanced technologies to enhance its working relationships with the retail trade. In developing markets, it is also applying advanced technologies, whenever it can, to the less sophisticated distribution systems of developing markets. When advanced technologies don't apply, ingenuity helps.

Some of the lessons learned in working with U.S. and Western European retailers are being applied directly to other countries that have large supermarket retailers. However, the retail distribution systems in many parts of the world are not even as efficient as the U.S. or European systems were a hundred years ago. Nevertheless, P&G works hard to apply modern tools and methods when working with these new customers.

In Poland, for example, eighty percent of packaged-goods volume sells through stores that in the U.S. would be called mom and pop stores, very small shops that move only a couple of units of most items a week, or a month. They don't need to be resupplied by an eighteen-wheeler. They don't even need full-size cases of, say, two dozen items. With the help of handheld computers to record and tally orders, and daily deliveries from small vans, and with the ability to resupply from broken cases, P&G is able to bring the efficiencies of automation and a sort of "just in time" delivery to the immature distribution system of this underdeveloped but growing market.

Mom and pop stores are also an important part of the retail distribution system in China. But these retail outlets make their own decisions about which brands to carry. So P&G takes street maps of the 228 Chinese cities with at least 200,000 citizens, pinpoints the locations of mom and pop shops, and sends in swarms of locally hired "ground troops," often wearing white sport shirts with "Winning Team" written on the back, to sell and service each outlet.

CHAPTER

5

HOW TO SUCCEED AS A P&G BRAND MANAGER

In most departments at P&G, it is the company's expectation and hope that its new hires will spend their careers at the company. A high level of performance is expected and encouraged. Employees are promoted on merit and on a when-ready basis. If they peak at one level and stop progressing, they are still valued and not asked to leave.

It's different in brand management. All the major brand decisions bubble up to top management through the brand management organization. The result, according to one former employee who started in product development before transferring over to brand management, is "a much higher level of intensity and competitiveness in brand management." As another put it, "the brand management culture feeds a certain amount of drivenness." There is an unwritten schedule for promotion for every level there and a very clear sense of "up or out."

Brand people feel an urgency to perform. They often stay late and work weekends. As one former P&G executive said, "Show a brand person a ruler and they will elbow each other out of the way to run up and measure themselves against it." Some of those who do not stay on track will find a good fit elsewhere in the organization. But most will have many other opportunities to choose from outside the company.

Brand management is not for everybody. But most of the lessons for success in brand management are applicable to just about any career.

LESSON 66

Be your consumer's advocate.

The brand manager who succeeds in marshaling the company's resources to delight the consumer will invariably succeed.

For two reasons. First, when the consumer embraces a brand, sales and share usually follow. Second, it's the best way to get things done in the P&G culture. When the consumer speaks, everybody listens. If the brand manager takes action because it's what the consumer wants, P&G people respond.

But it takes work to really get to know and understand your consumer. Brand managers go beyond studying all the consumer research reports; they observe research directly— observing focus groups, of course, but also listening in on telephone interviews. Some actually conduct the research. According to company lore, former CEO Howard Morgens spent months in the field going house to house to talk with consumers. Brand managers read the consumer mail. They observe consumers as they make their brand selections in the grocery store, and they often talk with them about why they made a particular selection and what was going through their minds. They also have access to a database of consumer research that relates to their brands. They can go into the database and run the data in different ways to explore questions or seek deeper insights.

LESSON 67 ———————————————

Learn the business.

The brand manager is expected to know more about his or her brand than anyone else in the company.

It might be difficult to learn more about your brand's chemistry than R&D knows or more about how your brand is selling in Peoria than the district sales manager knows or more about the cost of goods than purchasing knows. But you can certainly know more about your brand's chemistry than purchasing or sales knows and more about your brand's cost of goods than the district sales manager or R&D and more about your brand's sales in Peoria than R&D or purchasing.

And you had better make it your business to know more about your brand than your boss knows. Because, at P&G, your knowledge will be continually tested. Business conversations are fact-based conversations and *you* are expected to have the facts. Ed Artzt once asked the U.S. brand manager of Head & Shoulders what the incidence of dandruff was in China. The relevance of that knowledge to the issue at hand was not readily apparent, and at least one witness to the incident suspected there was another motive behind the question. The brand manager knew just enough to make an educated guess and escaped relatively unscathed. The point was reaffirmed: a thorough grasp of the business matters.

LESSON **68** ————————————————————

Make something happen.

No brand manager gets promoted at P&G without demonstrating initiative and business results. "Builds the business" is the first criterion of effective performance, and how the individual has gone about that task is the focus of any promotion recommendation.

One of the essential characteristics of the successful brand manager is the propensity to be a forceful advocate. A former marketing manager (the level above brand manager) stated, "It goes beyond a *willingness* [to make something happen]. It is the *need* to jump into a situation and take the reins."

Initiative is probably the most important characteristic P&G looks for in its candidates for brand management. Sure, intelligence and a well-rounded background are important. But those are price-of-entry minimums. When you're interviewed, if you are not ready to jump all over the question "What have you accomplished?" you will not be one of the candidates who gets an offer to join the company.

P&G recruiters don't simply interview whoever signs up

for on-campus interviews. They cultivate relationships with placement directors and marketing professors to help identify "hot" prospects. And they review the résumés of candidates who never thought about P&G. The primary quality the recruiters look for is a pattern of achievement. A track record of leadership, influencing other people, and making things happen is more important than a good GPA.

David Grocer's memory of his recruitment is telling. He was sought out by P&G prior to his graduation from the Kellogg Graduate School of Management. Following the on-campus interview, David was invited to Cincinnati. He had other job offers and had some reservations about P&G. He decided to confront P&G about them directly. At the end of an interview with a senior executive of the group he would ultimately join, he said, "I hear this rumor that all you guys do is write memos all day." The response was neither defensive nor confrontational: "David, if you are not going to come here and build the business, we don't want you." David said, "With that, my interest started to grow. They look for your leadership, thinking, and abilities to make things happen. And it turned out to be true. The memo thing was overblown. That's just the way they communicate and get things approved. But *you've* got to make it happen, not the memo."

LESSON **69** ─────────────

Lead by making others winners.

*Leadership is an important quality throughout the
company, and it takes on a special meaning in brand
management. The brand manager's success depends on his
or her ability to make things happen by getting the
cooperation and support of other people. The staff groups
that create the product, produce it, design the package,
create the promotions, and sell the product to the retail
trade do not report to the brand manager. The brand
manager has no authority to demand anything of any staff
group, but must prevail using whatever means
possible—usually by creating a win-win opportunity.*

Leadership in brand management means selling your
ideas to the people who make it happen.

Jay Stockwell had a leadership epiphany of sorts when
he joined P&G. Jay had a command-and-control concept of
leadership that was based on his seven years in the U.S.
Navy flying a P-3 and leading a support team of officers and
enlisted men. He was the boss, he called the shots, and, after
the support team's work was done, he did the flying. The
difference at P&G was "there's nothing you can do by yourself as a brand manager. Name one thing I can do sitting at
my desk that's going to ship a case out the door or add profit
to the bottom line. You absolutely and totally rely on everybody else. So I think the most critical success factor in
brand management is leadership. Sure you have to be able
to think and problem solve. Sure you have to be creative

and innovative. And you have to establish priorities. But you're dead in the water if you can't lead."

Cathy Risk Linder, a former assistant brand manager, believes that

> building allies and creating win-win situations was critical to success in brand management. You had to manage or direct people in other functional areas—market research, sales, the advertising agency, finance. Your boss and the managers up the line in brand management would step aside to see if you could do it. You didn't have authority, but you had influence. The brand groups were a window to top management for the staff groups.
>
> It's all the more remarkable when brand people earn the respect of the staff people because of the bias that exists. They assume you thought you were king of the world. Hub of the wheel and all that. There was resentment. And, if they didn't like you, they could sabotage your ideas by inaction.
>
> I remember a pet project of a brand manager that got absolutely nowhere. Whether or not it was a good idea, it didn't even get considered, because the product development manager hated the brand manager's guts. It's not just personalities *or* ideas *or* rank. It has to have merit *and* be sold.

Cathy cited Walter Solomon as a brand management superstar with a remarkable ability to work with other people. He was a "young, self-confident, savvy guy who broke barriers with his funny, friendly style. Even as a young brand assistant, he figured out how to throw himself into technical issues and be perceived as the leader of the project. This is remarkable because the technical group was not easily won over."

Walter was hired right out of undergraduate school and was promoted to brand manager at the age of twenty-five. He doesn't remember the specifics that so impressed Cathy with his performance as a brand assistant. But he clearly remembers the importance of getting support from others when he was promoted to brand manager of the Lilt home permanent brand.

Lilt home permanent was an old, tired brand. It was out of step with the hairstyles and habits of the time. Sales were in a long-term decline. Worse yet, Lilt was a small, orphaned brand. No one paid much attention to it, and management saw no reason to invest resources to build it.

Walter attacked his first brand assignment with vigor. He knew he would need to come up with new ways to think about the business and to enroll the support of others in the organization.

In reviewing the history of the brand, Walter realized that eighty percent of the sales had been in only a handful of retail accounts—accounts that had a significant presence in the more rural counties. Lilt had been an important brand to those accounts, but it was in decline even among them. Walter said he

> had to go enroll some of the sales people to pay attention to the smallest-volume brand in the shop. The big shampoo brands would make or break their quotas, not this dinky little home permanent. Together we sat down with customers like Wal-Mart and Dollar General stores who had a strong rural presence and asked them "If you wanted to drive this category, what can we do? Who should we talk to? What kind of advertising or promotion do we need?" Then I got Burnett [the ad agency Leo Burnett] to come along with us to get them out of Chicago and stop thinking about beautiful models and find out who Lilt's consumers really were and what their lives were all about. At first they weren't too enthusiastic about it because they didn't make any money on Lilt. But they began to see that we could do something with the brand, and they created a campaign that celebrated

good old-fashioned country people who had the gumption to do their own hair rather than go to a beauty parlor. We put together a marketing plan as a team, got it approved, and increased volume twenty percent in the following year. It was a win for everybody—it made an unexpected contribution to the sales guys' quota, it resulted in incremental volume for the accounts that had done well with the brand, and the television commercial that Leo Burnett produced won a P&G "World-Class Advertising" award—which matters a lot to Procter agencies, regardless of the size of the account.

Walter was given the added assignment of Pantene and was ultimately promoted to marketing manager responsible for the hair-care brands. By then, P&G was moving more aggressively into the global marketplace and was strategically focused on the more dominant brands with worldwide potential. Lilt was one of the first brands divested by the company as part of that strategy. Ironically, one of the last things Walter did before he left the company was to spearhead that divestiture effort.

LESSON **70**

Lead by helping others solve the problem.

Leadership can be manifested by defining the issue and facilitating the accomplishments of others.

Theresa Bannon was a freshly minted BA from the University of Notre Dame and only twenty-one years old when

she joined P&G as a brand assistant on Luvs disposable diapers.

As all new brand assistants do, she heard about how the
brand manager superstars "made their bones" and how
those-who-are-no-longer-with-us went down in flames. It
quickly became clear that, to Make Things Happen, she had
to work effectively with people in other departments who,
as she said,

> had been around a long time and knew a whole lot more
> than I did. I was kind of lucky. First, it's bad enough to
> be young and inexperienced. But to appear to be young
> and inexperienced *and dumb* to people who knew so
> much more than I did was a frightening thought. So I
> made it my business to do my homework and learn as
> much about the technical process, or whatever, that I
> could. Second, it wasn't in my nature to pretend I had
> the best solution to the problem. I truly welcomed their
> ideas, and I looked for opportunities to do what I could
> to help others.
>
> I particularly remember a performance review in
> which a guy in technical support, who was old enough
> to be my father, told my boss that I was one of the easi-
> est people he had ever worked with. He said I didn't pre-
> tend to know more than I knew. Two things made that
> performance review so memorable. First, that my boss
> thought it was such a big deal in the first place. I was
> just an inexperienced kid out of college doing what
> comes naturally. Second, that a very important part of
> my review was what the people in other departments
> told my boss about my effectiveness.

Theresa made others feel more productive. She was promoted two years and nine months after her arrival at P&G
and, at twenty-five, was one of the youngest brand managers in the company. Her assignment: to develop new prod-

uct and marketing opportunities for Always feminine hygiene products, leading a task force of people twenty years her senior.

LESSON **71** ————————————————

Be like Bobo.

Bobo is a nearly life-size plastic clown that has a weighted base. So you can punch Bobo and knock him over, but he will pop right up again. Successful brand managers exhibit Bobo-like resiliency.

A former marketing manager and thirteen-year veteran of brand management believes P&G's success with the brand management system has a lot to do with the recruitment of people who are "talented, motivated, and motivatable. These are people who, when you tell them their effort was not quite up to snuff, will redouble their efforts. They have a high need for approval and a need to succeed."

Ex-P&Ger Juelene Beck expresses the idea this way: "If your boss sends your recommendation back with comments, then he cancels the appointments you set up to review the memo seven times, you can't give up. It's up to you. If you have to wait until eight-thirty P.M. and walk him to his car [to get the time you need with him], that's what you do."

LESSON **72** ——————————————

Rules are for the obedience of fools and the guidance of wise brand managers.

The successful brand manager never breaks the law, but has been known to break a rule or two. If a rule or procedure or even a dictate from above is in conflict with Doing the Right Thing for a brand, the successful brand manager will find a way around, over, or through the barrier—at no small risk to his or her job. But consider the alternative. If abiding by a rule prevents the brand manager from being able to Do the Right Thing and Make Things Happen, the brand manager might as well begin looking for a new job anyway.

As a new brand manager on Crisco, Steve Dennis did his homework and made two early conclusions: the brand was declining, with no programs in place offering any hope for reversal, and consumers would respond to Crisco recipe ideas. Steve and his brand group came up with the idea of promoting Crisco recipes over the radio at a time of day when homemakers were deciding what to prepare for dinner. He also decided that he didn't have the six months or so that it would take to get approvals to do a "proper" test. So he did a "pilot test" with a local radio station in Cincinnati and got ten times the expected response. He didn't go up the chain of command to get the normal approvals for copy, production, and for buying media because it was only a "pilot test." But then, no one had ever heard of an advertising "pilot test" until Steve invented it. He presented the tape of the commercial and the results to his boss as "just a little pilot test here; hope it's okay," knowing full well that he had put his career in jeopardy. It went up the chain of command without challenge, and P&G ended up doing TV commercials based on the same concept. Through proper channels.

LESSON **73** ————————————————————

If you disagree with your boss, push back.

If you don't Make Something Happen because your boss won't let you, that's your problem. You make no progress, and you have failed as a leader. Or if your boss wants you to do something that you don't agree with, and it fails, that's also your problem. Be sure you're right, then push back.

P&G management has a relatively high tolerance for being challenged. The "push back" concept is encouraged. CEO John Pepper has written eloquently about how his management gave him his head during the course of his career. Ed Artzt wrote a memo about "how to be told no." As tough and as feared as he was, he supposedly loved it when his subordinates bucked him with a clear and compelling rationale for why his way was not the best way.

Gibby Carey, a former vice president of advertising, believes that the art of pushing back is an important element in the P&G culture:

> It's a subtle form of resisting management efforts to seize the initiative from the lower levels, where it prop-

erly belongs. P&G people take seriously the axiom, The game is lost when the coaches go in to play.

Many years ago, one of our brightest young men left the company to work for the Committee to Re-elect President Nixon. He didn't last there very long because the culture was so antithetical to everything he had learned at Procter. To question your management—to push back—amounted to being disloyal. And to be branded disloyal was death. He left the CRP shortly before Watergate. It was an appalling lesson of power abused. At P&G, the best ideas and the hardest data should prevail over the biggest initials. It happens at all levels.

Pushing back worked for Rich Wong when he was promoted to brand manager on Puffs facial tissue in the paper division. It was his good fortune that, shortly after he took over the brand, the product-development people came up with a line extension product that was relatively simple to produce. It was well received by the consumer in concept tests and in blind tests. Rich recommended immediate national launch since Kimberly-Clark could quickly replicate the product if the concept and product were exposed in a test market. The sales department eagerly supported the recommendation. "There was no way it would not pay out," Rich said.

But he had a problem. His boss would not approve the introduction until it was proven under standard test-market conditions. Rich's boss had been credited with a very successful product launch as brand manager in another division and had recently been promoted to marketing manager and transferred into the paper division. He was on a fast career track, but he was finding his way in a new division and had no reason to rock the boat. To call for a standard test market was certainly an unassailable decision in the

P&G manner. But in Rich's opinion, it was not Doing the Right Thing, under the circumstances.

Since the line extension had been a significant component of the annual plan, Rich insisted that he and his boss together review the issues with the general manager of the division. Rich had an opportunity to express his point of view. As a result the general manager approved the product's immediate introduction into a lead market for "ship test" purposes (to make sure there were no bugs in the manufacture and distribution of the product) immediately followed by a national launch. The introduction was successful, and there were no repercussions. It was the Right Thing To Do.

Rich adds that there was more at risk than his relationship with his boss and the obligation to Make Something Happen. His credibility with all the other departments was on the line. He had taken the lead on this project, as he should have. "The brand manager is the guy on the hook for business results," he said,

> and everybody in the organization knows it. So you're the leader, and you get everyone to invest their energies into the project. If you fold your cards and go home, you demotivate the entire organization—market research, sales, product development, manufacturing, your assistant brand managers—and they lose confidence in you to get things done, or your ability to push the right business ideas.
>
> If the point person in this tension-filled system doesn't play the role correctly, that's when bureaucracy creep starts to fill up empty space in the organization. So when Durk Jager [the COO] pronounces that he wants to see more sampling and advertising spending and that he doesn't like couponing or trade allowances anymore, and you're not allowed to do couponing and

trade allowances unless you get his personal sign-off, the politic thing to do is what Durk likes. But what if you don't have a noticeably superior product? You should put your money into trade allowances and couponing to hold on to distribution until you get the problem fixed. I know some brand people who were in that situation but they wouldn't ask for a sign-off and they nearly tanked the brand.

In other companies the brand manager is just the marketing guy doing advertising and positioning and consumer research and promotion. You have no power to go to the head of manufacturing or whoever made that decision and say, "I cannot have this," and get it changed. In the Procter environment, if you're doing your job, you go talk to whomever you have to and you garner enough support and take it up the line until you get it done. You can get exceptions to policies if it's the right thing to do.

LESSON 74 ─────────────────────────

Nurture the creative function.

Creativity is an important part of just about everything to do with the brand—particularly the packaging, advertising, and promotion. The brand manager depends heavily on others to generate creative ideas. The nurturing of the process is a critically important skill.

Creative ideas are subjective and are not easily evaluated by hardheaded analysis. Often a creative idea is fragile and vulnerable; its merit is not immediately recognizable and only becomes clear after some evolving of the idea or when it is executed in a more finished form. Therefore, many creative people feel vulnerable and are readily intimidated. Just the anticipation of a critical attack on a creative presentation can chill the creative process. P&G understands this and is careful not to let it happen.

"It is both a cultural and substantive piece of learning in the early days," says Paul Kadin of his indoctrination to evaluating copy as an assistant brand manager. "[There is a] way in which to interact with an agency to give feedback on creative things. Whether it's a package design or advertising campaign, there is a way to think about it that is designed to get your point across but also to make it acceptable to the creative people involved on the other side of the table. I still try to do it that way. [Judging from] what I see around me, there are very few people with that sensitivity. [But] whenever you're with a P&G person, they'll deal with it in a particular way."

The P&G feedback process (see the following illustration) typically starts with the elements of the creative work that seem to function well, and how they effectively execute the strategy and creative objectives. Then, starting with the most important things, an assessment is presented of what *doesn't seem* to work as effectively as it might and why. If the creator's intention is apparent, it should be appreciated and acknowledged. If there are redeeming or salvageable elements, this should be expressed, but without suggesting *how* the work should be changed. The person giving the feedback has to know when to stop. The three or four most important points are often enough. To point out every possible criticism can be demoralizing and counterproductive.

Fictional response of a P&G brand manager to an advertising agency's presentation of a new TV commercial storyboard for Zest bar soap.

[Overview statement following assistant brand manager's assessment.]

I agree with Linda that the storyboard is on strategy. Overall, it clearly conveys that Zest is an effective deodorant soap, no matter what your age, and that it rinses away easily.

[Cite three or four positive things.]

I think the demonstration is *particularly* effective. Lather on the glass of the shower stall in the shape of a Z for Zest rinsing off more easily than the S is terrific. It is a great visual and fits very naturally with the flow of the commercial.

The way you describe how the man washes his armpit in the shower should also be very effective.

And I think the casting, as you described it, will give the commercial some distinctivity, and that's good. That's been a problem for our advertising that you seem to have solved here.

Also, the tone of the interplay between the man and his wife in the opening of the commercial seems to be right on. It enables some tension in their dialogue as to whether or not Zest is the right choice, yet has an engaging charm.

[Cite three or four things that don't work or can be improved.]

I am a little concerned about *what* they are talking about in the opening, however. Although the double entendre of the pregnancy test is an ingenious idea, and is a good counterpoint to set up the bar soap issue, it takes us off in an unrelated direction. We know that commercials that get right into the problems or benefits that are relevant to our brands work well, and borrowed interest or double entendres in the opening have not generally been effective.

I'm also concerned that the opening takes quite a bit of time. We don't get to the product until about fifteen seconds into the commercial.

One last comment. I'm not sure that introducing the Zest body wash product at the end of the commercial works. It comes out of nowhere. If possible, we should leave the viewer with the regular Zest signature and a summation of what she or he just saw. Is there a way we could integrate the body wash in the main part of the commercial without interrupting the Zest bar soap story? Or maybe we should think about dealing with the body wash in separate advertising.

[Sum it up.]

I hope we can resolve these issues because there are some very good ideas here and, fundamentally, it could be a very distinctive and effective commercial.

LESSON **75**

Swashbucklers need not apply.

Entrepreneurship is often cited as a requisite characteristic of a brand manager at P&G. P&G admires this trait and looks for entrepreneurial initiative in the candidates it recruits. But entrepreneurs of the swashbuckler type do not typically do well in brand management at P&G.

Entrepreneurs generally are people who have a vision or a dream based largely on an intuition that is not always apparent to everyone around them—particularly not to people who are analytic and linear in their thought processes. Entrepreneurs often are not data-driven or detail-oriented. Some are flamboyant and can express their vision in compelling terms. They are typically creative, bold, intuitive, risk-taking people. Some lack patience and persistence— their initiative ebbs and flows with their sense of excitement about an idea. These are not characteristics commonly associated with the P&G brand manager.

A number of former P&G brand people who have been described as entrepreneurial types were not regarded as accomplished brand managers at P&G but have done extraordinarily well *after* they left P&G. Steve Ballmer, for example, left after a short, unnoteworthy stint at P&G to help his Harvard classmate and friend Bill Gates start Microsoft. Steve is executive vice president of Microsoft and has been described as "very sharp, but it's very hard to work under Steve because he was so random. . . . He's not a structured type of guy."

Scott Cook, who left P&G and created Intuit budgeting software, and Steve Case, who started America Online, have also been described by their contemporaries at P&G as entrepreneurial types who were not very comfortable at P&G. Steve Case's final memo at P&G decried the memo writing process as painstaking and unnecessarily exhaustive.

This is not to suggest that entrepreneurs cannot apply P&G's methods with some success. In fact, *Forbes* magazine profiled Scott Cook as an entrepreneur who applied the marketing arts he learned as an assistant brand manager selling Crisco to the marketing of Intuit's software products. The article quotes him as saying, "At Procter & Gamble, decisions are based on data, not judgment or whim," noting that he ran Intuit the same way.

LESSON **76** ————————————————————

Live by the code or get out of the game.

*A lot of brand management people perceive P&G as a
cultlike environment. They usually leave. Others find it
natural and comfortable.*

> Because the visionary companies have such clarity
> about who they are, what they're all about, and what
> they're trying to achieve, they tend to not have much
> room for people unwilling or unsuited to their de-
> manding standards.
>
> **—Collins and Porras,** *Built to Last*

Some embrace "The Procter Way" totally. They like their
peers because they are *like* their peers. And it's a good fit for
them personally. Most arrive in Cincinnati at the same time
as the rest of their "class." It's very natural for them to gravi-
tate to one another socially.

Others feel the "sameness" of the brand management social circles to be constraining and a threat to their individu-
ality. They want a greater sense of diversity in their social
world or a greater separation of their work life from their
social life.

Juelene Beck used to take off for Boston to go sailing
with friends when she was in brand management in the
1980s. And when she did stay in Cincinnati, she didn't go to
the parties or the usual haunts of her peers on Friday
nights. She enjoyed her non-P&G friends and would rather
do anything with them—such as go to the Sheep Shearing
Festival in nearby Kentucky—than go to the parties and activities that a lot of the other P&G brand people organized.

It bothered her that in a performance review her long-term commitment to P&G was questioned because of her outside interests.

Others, like Bruce Miller, "play the game." Bruce said he "was bemused, remote, and distant at first. I thought, 'These are a bunch of Moonies.' Showing up in the office at 'show time' on Saturday morning at 10 A.M. All they would talk about at parties was their brands. In fact, it's almost as if they *were* their brands. Tide, Bold, and Cheer were at the party. But as Lyndon Johnson said, 'It hurts good.' It was a badge. You were a part of something, and it was a challenge. So I said, okay, if that's the game, I'll play." Bruce was promoted to brand manager in less than the typical three years. Having won at "the Procter game," he left to "take a flyer in the entertainment field." That didn't work out, but he's glad he did it. "When I'm on my deathbed, I'll be glad I chased the dream rather than wonder about it," he said. Bruce now heads up Suissa Miller, a very successful advertising agency in Santa Monica, California.

P&G doesn't dictate what its employees should do outside the office—who they should socialize with, where they should live, or what kind of car they should drive. But there are some prevailing conventions inside the office.

In the past, those conventions more rigorously reflected the serious and purposeful demeanor of the P&G office environment than they do today. Several ex-P&G people tell of "suggestions" that their bosses have given them regarding "inappropriate" clothes and hairstyles. Then there's the story of a particularly hard-charging middle manager who was obviously overdue for a promotion. He was the only one in the office who wore a beard at a time when facial hair was incorrect. On a Wednesday he shaved it off. On Thursday, he was promoted. The message was not lost on the rest of the organization.

Today, the company spends much less energy enforcing such conventions. A lot of the men wear beards, and casual wear is now acceptable in the office. This doesn't mean that behavior and dress codes have disappeared. Behavior or dress that is distracting to the conduct of business or that makes "a statement" that protests the prevailing company conventions is not in the company's best interests. If you have a preference for purple-dyed hair or wear a nose ring, chances are brand management at P&G is not for you.

Although conventions such as the dress code have been relaxed, P&G is unabashedly conforming when it comes to the way business gets done. People are expected to get to work on time and put in a full, purposeful day. Brand managers are expected to work late. They are expected to provide the leadership to move the business forward and to continuously improve their personal performance. They are expected to conform to the P&G way of communicating with one another, to the P&G memo, to Doing the Right Thing, to Making Things Happen, and all the other parts of the P&G culture. It's a code of business conduct that is challenging and fulfilling for some people, and at least for those who are successful, there's a high level of conformity to it. It works at P&G. In fact, it is a code of conduct that can be highly effective in just about any business environment.

CHAPTER

6

GOING TO MARKET

When a new product comes out of the product development group, it is identified only by a code number. It is ready to be transformed into a brand. The process starts in earnest when a brand group is assigned.

Guided by a lot of consumer research, the brand group gives the product a name and a face (package). They determine where the brand will elbow its way into the existing competitive environment. They determine how they want the consumer to think and feel about the brand.

A marketing plan is developed: volume goals; a budget; advertising, media, and promotion strategies. The plan is tested in a test market. If the goals are achieved, the plan is expanded. Often the test-market experience leads to modifications to the plan and new test markets.

The process of learning about and refining the brand, responding to changes in its marketplace, and designing new ways to market the brand never ends.

TRANSFORMING THE PRODUCT INTO A BRAND

LESSON **77** ———————————————

Pick a simple, distinctive name.

The name becomes the brand, not the other way around.

> What's in a name? That which we call a rose by any
> other name would smell as sweet.
>
> —**Shakespeare,** *Romeo and Juliet*

Ivory, Crisco, Tide, Bold, Cheer, Crest, Pampers, Downy,
Cascade, Dawn, Prell, Zest—P&G brand names are typically
one or two syllables long, easy to pronounce, distinctive and
easy to remember. They often have connotations that may
help establish the benefit of the brand early in its life—such
as Downy, which connotes softness, and Pampers, which
connotes caring and comfort.

P&G stays away from generic names. Names that describe the product—such as Clean 'n' Mild—lack distinctiveness.

LESSON **78** —————————————————————

The package is the face of the brand.

The brand name logotype and the package design elements
combine to form the visual symbol of the brand. The
package is used as a signature in television and print
advertising, and it is what the consumer sees when
shopping in the grocery store. P&G packages are distinctive,
readily identifiable, and uncluttered.

Don Baker, who headed up P&G's package design group
for many years, put it this way: "It's the face of the brand,
the memorable thing. When you mention the brand, [the
consumer] thinks of the package, so you have to be careful
about changing it. You've got to have a face for the brand so
they instantly recognize it on the shelf."

P&G also looks for design elements consistent with the
brand's positioning. The Tide graphics connote power and
heavy duty. The baby on the Pampers and Charmin packages suggests gentle softness. The shape of the Mr. Clean
bottle echoes the cross-armed stance of the Mr. Clean character and is suggestive of the strength of the product.

Some brands use words, or "blurbs," to convey a more
explicit statement related to their positioning, such as Charmin's "squeezably soft" or Bounty's "the quicker picker
upper." But most P&G packages refrain from "sell copy" on
the packaging.

The brand name logotypes of P&G packages are always
easy to read; if they are superimposed on other design elements, they are outlined in white (for dark logotypes) or
black (for white logotypes). The design elements are usually
quite simple, with a limited number of bold colors.

LESSON **79** ———————————————

Design for shelf impact.

*A single package by itself can look very different from a lot
of the same packages side by side. When P&G gets close to
a final package design, it will make up several package
"facings" and see how they look on the shelf—to assure that
they stand out versus clusters of competitive packages.*

Bold colors, simple graphics, and uncluttered packaging
all contribute to an impactful multiple-package visual effect. The package graphics of Head & Shoulders, Pert Plus,
and Bounty towels are good examples. A dominant color
can have the same effect. Next time you are in a grocery
store, notice how the orange of Tide's packaging jumps out
from the blur of other colors on detergent packages. Or how
the blue packaging of the Always brand stands out in the
feminine hygiene section. Or how the white background ties
together the Crest line of products.

Sometimes the desire for shelf impact comes into conflict with the need to be consistent with the brand's positioning. In Don Baker's words: "You've got to have shelf
impact. But sometimes that's hard to do when you're dealing with a soft product like a perfume or hand lotion. Or
toilet tissue or facial tissue, which is trying to connote softness."

Shelf impact considerations also come into play when
designing for the different versions of a brand. The goal is
to maintain an overall commonality of dominant visual elements but, at the same time, make it easy for the consumer
to distinguish among the versions.

LESSON **80** ─────────────────────

Find the consumer insight.

Product performance is only the starting point of the development of the marketing and advertising strategies. Consumer insights help determine how to communicate the brand's benefits in the most meaningful and believable way, and which consumers would be most receptive.

There's nothing wrong with a straightforward presentation of a brand's benefits, or with hammer-it-home advertising such as the classic Anacin "For Fast! Fast! Fast relief!" campaign. Some P&G advertising is very straightforward in its presentation of the brand's performance benefits.

However, consumer insights can lead to more engaging or exciting ways to communicate a brand's benefits. Finding the insights means finding consumers' "hot buttons." Focus groups are frequently used to do this.

What's the best way for the consumer to think about the benefit of your brand?

Research might suggest, for example, that the typical fabric softener user is a housewife and mother who works hard to do everything she can for her family. This might make the Downy fabric softener brand group and its advertising agency cautious about portraying an independent, self-sufficient supermom in their advertising. Instead they might want to consider having the husband in their commercial touch his wife's arm or express some other assurance that she is loved and appreciated. The insight that

Downy gives the homemaker the opportunity to feel she is doing something extra for her family is at the heart of Downy's advertising today.

Jif peanut butter uses the best peanuts to bring out more fresh-roasted taste than any other leading creamy brand. Do kids really care? What's important is the insight that Moms care what their kids eat, and choosing Jif can be perceived as being a better mom.

Pantene shampoos and conditioners rejuvenate hair. The insight is that shiny hair is a much-desired attribute and shininess is associated with healthy hair. All over the world, Pantene is "for hair so healthy it shines."

VapoRub ointment relieves chest colds. VapoRub can also be the catalyst for a caring, loving interaction between mother and child. VapoRub is advertised as "Touch therapy—Vicks VapoRub puts it in your hands."

To which consumer segment is your brand most likely to appeal?

Oil of Olay is not about looking younger; it's about looking great at whatever age you are. The advertising empathizes with middle-aged women in a reassuring way that makes them feel comfortable about who they are.

It wasn't until P&G targeted teenagers with the "Once you pop, you can't stop" advertising campaign that Pringles took off. The campaign enabled consumers to think about the product in a different way—as a good-tasting, contemporary product that's fun to eat.

How can you get consumers to *believe* that your brand does what you say it does?

Some consumer insights can be used to get consumers to *believe* that the benefit claimed by the brand is really true.

For example, years ago P&G added bleach crystals to Oxydol detergent, which it colored green. The green coloration did not add any functionality to the product. But P&G had the insight that the consumer needed some indication that the product was different. The crystals were added as a form of marketing communication to help the consumer understand what the brand was all about—getting clothes cleaner and whiter.

Credibility is even more important for products with benefits that are less discernible to the consumer, such as a cavity-prevention toothpaste. You can't see cavity prevention or feel it, and you have no way of knowing whether it works until you have used the product for an extended period of time. So why should you believe the claims for one product versus those for competing brands claiming similar benefits?

Obtaining the American Dental Association's endorsement of the cavity-prevention benefit of Crest toothpaste (as described in the following discussion) is a classic example of the importance of establishing the credibility of claims for products whose performance is less discernible.

Through a coordinated effort between Indiana University research scientists and P&G, a stannous fluoride toothpaste product was developed that reduced the incidence of children's cavities by nearly half. It was a remarkable consumer-product triumph. The product was introduced as Crest toothpaste.

Crest went into test markets in 1955 and achieved a twelve percent share of market—enough to justify national expansion but disappointing for such a significant product advance that provided such an important and appealing benefit. Furthermore, the "Look, Ma, no cavities!" advertising campaign, with Norman Rockwell drawings, clearly communicated the product's benefit and achieved widespread attention. The problem was that consumers had no reason to believe the benefit versus similar competitors' claims. Although competitors did not have access to the patented stannous fluoride formula of Crest, they made similar promises of cavity reduction with the launch of numerous compounds containing sodium fluoride. Crest settled out nationally at a ten percent share.

P&G had submitted its clinical tests to the ADA at about the same time Crest toothpaste went into test markets. John Smale is largely credited with securing the ADA endorsement a full six years later. The endorsement enabled the consumer to believe the cavity-prevention promise and to establish a relationship with the brand. Sales tripled and Crest surpassed Colgate as the leading toothpaste brand in the U.S.

ENTERING THE MARKETPLACE

LESSON **81** ——————————————

Plan to dominate.

Dominance is a practical issue. Dominant brands are usually the most profitable brands because advertising and administrative expenditures are prorated over a larger volume of product. Dominant brands have a stronger presence and credibility with the consumer, and the retail trade prefers to feature leading brands.

Dominance is also a philosophical issue. Some companies are primarily focused on the efficiency of the marketing investment. They seek to spend up to the point of diminishing returns to maximize the return of each dollar invested. For P&G, the issue is "How high is up?" P&G will invest heavily to achieve leadership. The investments often don't pay off for years.

It's also an attitudinal issue. If P&G starts with a superior product, doesn't it deserve to be the market leader? Anything less is a failure of marketing. Dominance is winning.

In a speech to the Association of National Advertisers, Wolfgang Berndt, the current executive vice president for North America, expressed the willingness of the company to invest heavily in a brand, based on his personal involvement with the introduction of Ariel in Austria. Typical of most

P&G brand introductions, home-delivered product sampling was part of the introductory program. Sampling is an extremely expensive marketing tool, so sampling was limited to about forty percent of all homes—the homes of only those consumers who were thought most likely to become loyal users of the brand. The sampling program was extraordinarily successful, so P&G sampled an additional twenty percent of homes. That worked too, and P&G did not stop until nearly one hundred percent of all the homes in the market were sampled. It wasn't the most efficient marketing program, but it was the most effective. Ariel became the dominant brand.

For other companies, marketing is more likely to be viewed as a pay-as-you-go proposition. There's less up-front investment spending, so there's less need for exhaustive test marketing and fine-tuning of the marketing plan before launching the brand nationally. And the leverage of marketing activities—the return on every marketing dollar invested—is more important than dominance.

LESSON **82** ─────────────────

Plan to be first.

*The first brand into a product category usually becomes the
leading brand. Xerox, Coca-Cola, Kleenex, and Advil were
the pioneer brands in their categories and are practically
generic brand names. Tide, Pampers, Crest, and Comet were
pioneer brands and enjoy leadership positions—in the
minds of consumers and in terms of market share.*

*P&G is proactive. P&G wants to invent things that never
existed before. It wants to develop product improvements
and be first to market them.*

In order to protect the advantage of being first into the
marketplace, P&G is very secretive and cautious about
exposing its ideas or plans. Steve Stoller recalls the extraordinary security surrounding the testing of Tide Sheets, his
first assignment as assistant brand manager. Tide Sheets
was a product, similar to Bounce in form, that was impreg-
nated with detergent, bleach, and fabric softener. The brand
group operated out of an office that was locked when it
wasn't being used. There were no trash cans; only shred-
ders. P&G shipped the product from the plant to a test facility in unmarked trucks followed by security guards.
Ultimately, all the secrecy didn't matter; the consumer rejected the product in test market.

P&G buys time by testing an idea as much as it can *before* exposing it to competition in an actual test market. In
addition to conducting product and concept tests with the
consumer, it makes extensive use of simulated market tests

in which consumers have the opportunity to buy a product in a simulated grocery store setting at a research facility.

Occasionally, P&G *will* take calculated risks in order to be first in the marketplace.

Ex-P&Ger John Calhoun recalls an experience that demonstrates the importance of being first to P&G. It is also a good example of how the brand management system works.

> We had developed a Bounce-with-stain-guard line extension of the brand which was not doing well in its first months in test markets. As the assistant brand manager, I was given the assignment to figure it out—with some coaching from my brand manager.
>
> I found there were some fundamental things about the product that didn't align with the marketing plan. For example, it takes several uses of the product for the stain protection to build up on clothing, so the benefit is not noticed right away. But when we did focus groups among users who had used the product for several months, they said "Wow, I've noticed that stains have come out that I didn't think would come out."
>
> Since the test-market marketing plan included only a one-sheet sample, we concluded that we needed to build in additional trial incentives and run a more sustained advertising effort. It was a more expensive plan, and it was untested. But we recommended we go national with it because we were in an intense rivalry with Lever's Snuggle fabric softener at the time, and they were making some inroads. They had plenty of time to develop their own stain-guard product. If we didn't go national, we would have lost our chance to be first in the marketplace and regain our leadership of the category. One by one, people up the line got on board with the recommendation and, interestingly, as each person got on board, he was the next champion of the recommendation to take it forward. We went national and, a year later, had over a fifty percent share of market.

LESSON **83** ──────────────────

It's better to be right than to be first.

Since a lot of money is invested in a national introduction
of its brands, P&G wants to eliminate as much risk as
possible before the brand is introduced nationally. The
company is exhaustively thorough in all phases of up-front
planning. When P&G introduces the brand in test markets,
typically the brand is kept there until success is virtually
assured.

> This kind of organization creates an environment in
> which it is possible that a good idea may sometimes
> get lost, but it is one in which bad ideas seldom sur-
> vive.
>
> **—Brad Butler, former P&G chairman**

Every once in a while, P&G will expand nationally before
the brand is conclusively proven to be a success in test market—as it did with Bounce-with-stain-guard. But those are
exceptions to the rule. Other premature expansions out of
test markets have served as expensive reminders to be cautious.

For example, in 1983 P&G tested a line of Duncan Hines
soft cookies in Kansas City. Within a few months, P&G had
captured over thirty percent of the market in the test areas.
P&G expanded nationally, but Nabisco got there first with a
fifteen-flavor line of soft cookies called Almost Home. As a
result, Nabisco's total national cookie share jumped to
thirty-six percent, leaving Duncan Hines soft cookies with
only a five percent share of the national market. Should
P&G have gone national sooner in order to be the first

brand in the market? No. It should not have gone national at all. Consumers soon went back to crunchy chocolate chip cookies, and soft cookies became one of recent history's biggest passing fads. Neither Duncan Hines soft cookies nor Nabisco's Almost Home are on the market today.

P&G had a similar experience with Pringles. When the brand took off in its test market, the company committed to capital expenditures for national expansion. About nine months after the brand's national introduction, the novelty wore off and sales began a long-term slide that lasted for several years. P&G had overreacted to the brand's early success and had failed to stay in the test market phase long enough to see the effects of taste fatigue. Even though the brand was eventually successful, the national introduction at that time was a very expensive mistake.

LESSONS FOR EFFECTIVE TELEVISION ADVERTISING

P&G believes that the following are the critical factors of effective television advertising:

- Recall—P&G commercials are typically linear, very easy to understand, and very easy to remember. For years P&G used day-after-recall testing as the sole measure of commercial effectiveness. Recall is still an important measure of advertising effectiveness because it is hard to persuade the consumers of anything if they can't remember the brand and the message. However, P&G now believes that recall alone does not necessarily translate into sales.

- Trial Potential—The best possible response to a commercial is for the consumer to want to run out and buy the brand. Trial potential is predicted by a purchase intention measure administered before and after consumers' exposure to the test commercial.

- Convincingness and Distinctiveness—P&G listens carefully to what viewers say about its test commercials. Consumers tend to respond well to commercials they describe as "convincing," "appealing," "makes me want to try it," "clever," "amusing," "realistic," "not stupid," "not silly," or "not the same old thing."

LESSON **84**

Be blatant about the benefit.

The consumer benefit is at the heart of every P&G commercial. The benefit should be clear and obvious, and every part of the commercial should enhance communication of the benefit.

The benefit of the current Folgers coffee campaign is clear from the beginning of the commercial and is explicit right through to the end when it is summed up in the tag line, "The best part of waking up is Folgers in your cup." A typical commercial opens to a man waking up and cuts to scenes of the can being opened and of coffee being scooped out of the can and brewed. As the man gets up, he smells the aroma and smiles in anticipation of the taste and stimulation of the coffee. There's a shot of coffee beans from "some of the world's richest coffee regions" to help explain why the coffee is so good. Then the man joins his family and/or friends to enjoy the coffee in a pleasurable social context, which, of course, is a pleasant part of waking up too. Every scene in the commercial contributes to the expression of an enjoyable waking-up experience.

P&G uses imagery in its commercials; the Folger's commercial is loaded with imagery. However, it uses imagery in support of benefits—not in place of them. So-called image advertising attempts to create an aura about the brand or to encourage consumers to identify themselves with the products or with their perception of other users of the products. So-called image advertising is less direct than most P&G advertising. Nike, for example, pays millions of dollars just to associate the brand with well-known athletes. No benefit is explicitly expressed in the Nike commercials. They don't talk about the brand or even show the product or a package—just the "Nike swipe" at the end of the commercial. It's not necessarily wrong for Nike. But P&G does it differently.

LESSON **85** ————————————————

Jump-start the commercial with a good "Hey, you!"

*The commercial break is often a good time for a bathroom
break, to see what is on another channel, or just to let the
mind wander. The opening of the commercial should
immediately engage those viewers you want to reach. And it
should be directly relevant to the benefit or to the problem
that the benefit solves.*

P&G commercials typically open with a verbal statement
of a problem or a situation that needs to be resolved or a
challenge—a premise that is relevant to the audience the
commercial wants to reach. The verbal opening line is usually the critical part of the opening. The visual part of the
opening plays an important supporting role by engaging the
viewer through eye contact with the homemaker or an-
nouncer who is speaking or with a scene related to whatever
is being said in a voice-over. It doesn't take long to know
what is going on. A sampling of opening lines follows.

OPENING LINES OF P&G TV COMMERCIALS

"As the youngest girl in my family, I grew up with a lot of hand-me-downs." (Tide)

"We're in Atlanta for the Gain 'Show and Smell' challenge." (Gain)

"My family wrote the book on stains." (Ultra Biz)

"Every time you have clothes to dry, you're putting Downy's softness to the test." (Downy)

"I'm happy you're doing the dishes, but you're doing them wrong." (Dawn)

"Oh! Ugly dirt! But I know who to call." (Mr. Clean)

"The Vidal Sassoon Academy with news you can use on styling damage. If your hair does this . . ." (Vidal Sassoon)

"U.S. Gold Medalist Mia Hamm spends 90 minutes destroying her hair. And 90 seconds bringing it back." (Pert Plus)

"Hey Annie!"
"Hi."
"Love the hat."
"I need it. My hair's a disaster. Look at my dandruff." (Head & Shoulders)

"Know what I used to hate about hair spray? Everything!" (Pantene)

"If you ever tried one of those clear antiperspirants, you know there's something missing." (Secret)

"All across America, we asked families to trade their soap for a breakthrough in family skin care. New Moisture Care from Ivory." (Ivory)

"So many products promise to stop wrinkles. So which should you use?" (Oil of Olay)

"I kept getting pimples. So I used every kind of soap I could find. But my face was still oily. Still dirty." (Clearasil)

"Life is complicated. Makeup shouldn't be." (Cover Girl)

"What's the one part of your body that can never be too fat? Your eyelashes!" (Max Factor)

"Think about it. The minty mouthwash that tastes a little too mediciny can leave your breath smelling a little too mediciny." (Scope)

"Glamorous Hollywood? Not to me. For me it's long hours and strange locations. Can't get slowed down by irregularity." (Metamucil)

"Unfortunately, these women had an overnight flight. And a cough." (Vicks Cough Syrup)

"You've always known how your touch can comfort your child. Now scientists have given it a name. Touch therapy." (Vicks VapoRub)

"I thought I knew the rules for better protection. The thicker the pad the better. Boy, was I wrong." (Always)

"Don't you wish you could get the soothing, gentle cleaning of a bath every time you change your baby?" (Pampers Baby Fresh)

"For really tough messes, you don't want to use a sponge." (Bounty)

"In my family we're always cooking. It's my way of expressing myself." (Crisco Oil)

"What do you think of those chips?"
"Chips? I love chips."
"They're good though, huh?"
"They're great chips."
"They're fat free."
[Laughs] "Yeah. Right." (Pringles)

LESSON **86** —————————————————————

Emphasize the solution, not the problem.

In a problem–solution commercial, the problem should be a problem the consumer can relate to and should be used only to set up the solution that the brand provides. Don't make the mistake of dwelling too long on the problem or of using such a dramatic problem that it overpowers the commercial.

Most P&G commercials spend only as much time with the problem as is necessary to set up the solution or the benefit. Occasionally when commercials are not working, the fault is too much emphasis on the problem or the problem is not particularly relevant.

For example, a Bounce fabric softener commercial achieved high recall by showing amusing situations of people dealing with the problem of static in their clothes. However, the commercial was not performing in the marketplace. P&G fixed the problem by revising the commercial to deemphasize the problem of static in clothes and emphasize the static-free clothing that resulted from using Bounce.

In an example of an irrelevant problem, a Spic and Span commercial that featured the problem of food stuck under the burner of the stove got a very good day-after-recall test score but did not perform well at all in the marketplace. The brand group and advertising agency conducted some diagnostic one-on-one interviews with consumers and concluded that the problem featured in the commercial was not relevant to consumers. They regularly cleaned under the burners of their stove so that such a problem was unlikely to occur, and they felt that anyone who did not was not a good housekeeper.

LESSON **87** ────────────────────────────

Show the package in the first eight seconds.

The brand should be registered in the viewer's mind before the benefits are presented. A review of recent thirty-second TV commercials for fifty-one P&G brands advertised in the U.S. showed that seventy-five percent of the commercials identified the brands within eight seconds.

Twenty percent of the commercials reviewed introduced the brand right at the outset of the commercial or within five seconds. Most of the commercials delayed introducing the brand until the problem or the set-up of the commercial situation was established in the opening, which, for P&G commercials, doesn't take much time. A few of the commercials inset the brand logo in the lower part of the screen right at the outset of the commercial.

LESSON **88** ────────────────────────────

Link the brand to the story of the commercial.

Look for opportunities to link the brand to the commercial, so that the story of the commercial—and the benefit of the brand—will not be confused with any other brand.

Introducing the brand early in the commercial is one way to accomplish this objective. Showing and repeating the name of the brand several times helps. Using the name in a unique way can help—such as using the nickname "Sunny D" for Sunny Delight; or using the name in the tag line, as in "Only Downy does it"; or "It's cleaner. It's drier. It's Always"; or "Pamper the skin they're in." Some commercials build the brand name into the demonstration, such as one for Zest in which soap film on a shower door in the shape of the letter Z rinses clean, while the S, for soap, does not.

P&G commercials rarely mention competitors by name. Doing so risks allowing viewers to confuse the brand names and associate the competitive brand with the benefits expressed in the commercial. P&G demonstrations refer to competitive brands as "the leading liquid detergent with bleaching power," "a premium detergent," "other leading liquid," or "regular shampoo," and so forth.

If the commercial has an identifiable personality or character associated with the brand, there is an opportunity to link the character and the end result. The reflection of Mr. Clean in the shine of the countertop or the floor is a good example. Mr. Whipple squeezing the Charmin indelibly linked the softness benefit to the Whipple character.

LESSON **89** ──────────────

Let the viewer *see* the benefit.

Approximately forty percent of the P&G commercials reviewed used side-by-side comparisons of the end result for the P&G product versus for the competition. Most of the other commercials show the benefit standing alone or conceptualize it with an animated graphic.

────────────────────────

Usually, the end-result comparison is visible and the superior performance of the P&G brand is obvious. The clothes cleaned in Tide were cleaner and brighter than the clothes cleaned in "the leading liquid detergent with bleaching power." The hair washed in Head & Shoulders had no dandruff; the hair washed with "regular shampoo" was loaded with dandruff. The Bounty towel held up; the "ordinary paper towel" disintegrated. Pampers and Always show side-by-side demonstrations of how much liquid can be absorbed by the P&G product compared to competitive products.

Occasionally, the difference isn't quite so apparent and needs a little help. It's hard to see that the towel washed in Downy is really softer than the one treated with "mid-priced softener," but a hand caressing the towel washed in Downy helps to make the point.

P&G uses side-by-side "demonstrations" even when the superiority of the P&G brand is not visible at all. For Pampers Baby Fresh wipes, P&G uses an *illustration* "at forty times magnification" to compare the evenly spaced fibers of Pampers Baby Fresh wipes with the clumps of fibers and "coarse bits of the other leading brand." For Bounty towels, it is impossible to show the actual germs that a sponge leaves behind compared to the clean swipe made by the Bounty towel. So the germs were conceptualized by some blue and green dots superimposed where the sponge swiped.

Many of P&G's commercials show the benefit without a side-by-side or before-and-after comparison:

- The Gain commercials visualize clean clothes by showing a housewife smelling articles of clothing.
- The benefit of Pantene is dramatized by showing shining hair cascading over a model's shoulder or from her hands.
- Pringles dramatizes the crispness of its chips with crackling sound effects.
- Folgers commercials visualize the aroma and taste of the coffee by showing the vacuum can being opened, the coffee grounds being spooned out of the can, the steam from brewing coffee or from the cup, and the smelling and tasting actions of the people in the commercials.
- Downy visualizes softness by showing people being cocooned in oversized, soft towels and a shot of the package bouncing on a stack of soft towels.

LESSON **90** ————————————————

Show the product in action, but don't get tangled up in the technology.

P&G doesn't make the mistake of focusing its commercials on the genius of the product's technology. Some P&G commercials will allude to a brand's technology to support the credibility of the promise, but those allusions are abbreviated, easy to understand, and directly in support of the benefit. Consumers want some assurance that the benefit is real, but they don't want a detailed explanation of the technology.

P&G's shampoo-and-conditioner-in-one technology is a stunning achievement in which the conditioner is held in suspension until the hair is rinsed. The Pert Plus commercial visualizes the shampoo-and-conditioner-in-one combination by showing a Pert Plus bottle displacing separate shampoo and conditioner bottles. The assertion that a single product can replace two products that the consumer has become accustomed to using might be met with some skepticism. An explanation is provided by a simple animated graphic symbolizing the suspended conditioner that coats the hair during the rinse. Without elaborate explanation, it signals to the viewer that there is something special about the product that makes it different from conventional separate shampoos and conditioners that enables it to deliver on its promise.

Similarly, for hair spray with P&G's Elastesse technology, a simple animated graphic shows how hair strands are bonded where they intersect, like spot welds, rather than along the entire length of the strands. This makes it readily understandable how Elastesse provides a "flexible hold" rather than the "helmet head" effect of conventional hair sprays.

Some Pantene commercials show an animated graphic of vitamins penetrating the hair from root to tip. In the same graphic, the hair shaft transforms from dull to shiny as the shaft is penetrated, thus directly linking the benefit to the visualization of how the product works.

LESSON **91** ──────────

Show what you say; say what you show.

It's difficult for the eye and the ear to operate independently. In P&G commercials, the audio and video are tightly connected. They call it "audio-video sync."

Some examples of audio-video sync:

- As Bounce fabric softener commercials promise "time release freshness that stays up to five days," they show freshness "bubbling up" out of the fabric day after day. Obviously, "freshness" doesn't literally bubble out of the fabric. No matter. It's a mnemonic visual that symbolically connects product performance to the benefit being promised.
- A Pampers Baby Fresh wipes commercial shows the words "natural fibers" dissolving into the sheet, accompanied by a voice-over talking about natural fibers.

- A Crest commercial shows animated bubbling action between teeth with the voice-over saying, "Its foaming action penetrates even the tiny crevices a toothbrush can't reach."

Rarely will you hear a statement in a **P&G** commercial that isn't supported by a compatible visual, even if the visual is the words that are being stated. Notice how tightly the audio and video track in the following **Pampers** commercial:

AUDIO	VIDEO
(Female Announcer) Every night when you put her to bed, you know she has a long night ahead of her.	Baby sleeping in crib. Baby turns over.
The last thing you want waking her up is clammy skin.	Baby waking up, crying. Mother picks her up, feels moisture on baby's bottom.
That's why there's Pampers Baby Dry.	Cut to package.
Its special baby-dry layers absorb faster than the leading regular diaper.	Side-by-side demo of liquid being poured into "leading regular" and "Pampers."
And Pampers helps your baby's skin feel dry. Even in the morning.	Close-up of mother's fingers caressing baby's bottom. Smiling mother with happy baby in morning.
Hospitals know dry skin is important to skin health, and 81% of them use Pampers.	"Dry skin is important to skin health." "81% of hospitals use Pampers."
Make them happy. Keep them dry. Pampers Baby Dry.	Laughing baby with mother. Package superimposed with: "Make them happy. Keep them dry."

LESSON **92** ——————————————

Use real people, not celebrities.

Use people with whom the desired audience can empathize.
These can be actors portraying consumers with whom the
viewer can identify, or they can be actual consumers. In
either case, viewers can more readily internalize the
satisfaction of people with whom they can identify.

Being a good mom is what the Jif commercial is all about. Because "Choosy Moms choose Jif." The benefit is explicitly conveyed in scenes of happy interaction of a mother with her child.

The benefit of Cover Girl cosmetics is evident in the confident, cool, in-control attitude of the "easy, breezy, beautiful" young women in the Cover Girl commercials.

Pringles potato chip commercials show people—mostly kids—not only enjoying the crunch and the taste of the potato chips but enjoying the whole process of eating them in a fun, social context. The commercials invariably cut to a quick scene of a rather pathetic, lonely soul struggling with broken, greasy bagged potato chips.

P&G occasionally uses professionals, such as a makeup artist for Max Factor or real-life athletes whose activities torture their hair before they use Pert Plus. However, the purpose is to give the commercials credibility, rather than to borrow interest from the recognition of the personality.

LESSONS FOR EFFECTIVE PRINT ADVERTISING

LESSON **93** ————————————————

Use an interesting visual.

Consumers flipping through pages of a magazine aren't looking for ads; according to research conducted by Roper Starch Worldwide, half the readers of women's magazines don't even notice the average packaged-goods ad. But if they see a picture or graphic that is of interest, they may stop to see what it is about.

Most P&G advertisements have a single, dominant visual. Often, the visuals enable the readers to see themselves in the ad. Ads for Clearasil, Always, Noxzema, Oil of Olay, Pantene, Vidal Sassoon, and other brands show people with whom the consumers of those kinds of products can identify and empathize—people they resemble or people they wish to be like. Mothers can readily empathize with the mother playing with her daughter and the headline "Being a mom . . ." in the Jif peanut butter ad. New mothers are attracted to visuals of babies in Dreft and Pampers ads; young women aspire to the look of beautiful models.

But there are other ways P&G engages people's interest with brand- or product-related visuals:

- In most of the Mr. Clean ads, it's hard not to notice the Mr. Clean character staring you in the eye.
- A Pringles ad shows a page full of pairs of Pringles

chips facing each other so they look like duck's bills, which makes the consumer want to stop to read what that's all about.

- An Always sanitary napkin ad that runs in *Seventeen* magazine engages the young teenage reader with cartoonlike pictures of cheerleaders (some jumping around, but one looking very much out of sorts because, obviously, she doesn't use the product). It *looks* as if it would be fun to read the captions about what they are saying.

LESSON 94 _____

Put the benefit in the visual.

Most P&G ads tell the story with the visual.

If you see a woman with shiny hair and a bottle of Pantene shampoo, you get the message. Same with a picture of a baby's bottom and a box of Pampers. Or a close-up visual of a man and woman with their smiling mouths about an inch apart and a bottle of Scope.

Metaphorical visualizations are not as compelling as actual end-result visualizations, but they can be an effective way to communicate when you can't literally visualize the benefit or how the product works. An ad introducing "mountain spring scented Tide" shows outdoor visuals with related captions: "crisp mountain air," "clean mountain snow," "fresh wildflowers," "bright sunshine and cool breezes." An Always feminine napkin ad shows a woman lounging on her bed. The headline says, "From day to night, your body position is different. Why isn't your pad?"

LESSON ## 95 ————————————————————

Connect the headline to the visual.

Sometimes an interesting visual needs a headline to help the story. Even if the visual tells the story all by itself, a headline can amplify the message.

- Pantene with Elastesse hair spray is designed to eliminate the "helmet head" effect of hair sprays. An ad for Pantene shows a woman joyously running her fingers through her hair. The headline, "This is the hair spray to have if you hate hair spray," completes the story.
- An ad for Crest toothpaste showing a "heroic" life-size picture of the Crest package conveys the anticavity message with the simple headline, "Metal Deflector."
- The Scope ad with the close-up of the mouths of the man and woman doesn't really need a headline. But the words "This ain't gonna happen if your minty mouthwash smells too mediciny" amplify the message.

LESSON **96** ————————————————————

Demonstrate the product.

Show a product's performance "in action."

- Dawn dish-washing liquid shows before-and-after photos of a greasy pot that has become sparkling clean after being washed with Dawn.
- Ultra Biz shows a side-by-side "demonstration" of overalls washed in Biz (which got the stains out) versus overalls washed in "the leading color-safe bleach" (which, not surprisingly, did not get the stains out).

Even representative artwork or drawings can convey how a product works:

- A Bounty towels ad shows a side-by-side visualization of a sponge cleaning up messy food spills on a high-chair tray. As in the television commercial, green dots are drawn on the tray to convey that the sponge leaves germs. No green dots have been added where the Bounty towel wiped.
- Pampers wipes ads show a baby's bottom to symbolize soft, dry, diaper rash–free skin. To be more specific about the promise, they conceptualize the benefit by an inset drawing showing a glow, representing a shield protecting the baby's bottom, and droplets of moisture that are unable to penetrate the glow.

LESSON **97** ─────────────

Keep the advertisement short and sweet.

Very few readers read body copy. The less copy you have, the better the chances of it being read.

P&G brand managers are not immune to the temptation to tell more than the reader really wants to know. However, most P&G ads manage to stick to a single message, and the median word count (including headline, body copy, and tag line) is approximately seventy words. Some of the most striking ads have considerably fewer words:

- A Cheer ad shows a bright, lime-green shirt dominating the page with a label that uses only six words, "Help keep limes lime. Wash in Cheer."
- The Pantene Gold Cap–collection ad is a two-page spread that features a woman with glorious golden hair. It uses only nineteen words: "Glistening. Gleaming. Glorious. Gold. The Pantene Gold Collection. Experience it for yourself. Pantene. For hair so healthy it shines."
- P&G's Hugo Boss perfume for women ad has eight words: "Life's a journey. Travel light. Don't imitate. Innovate."

LESSON **98** ——————————————

Give the reader permission to believe.

The primary goal of P&G print advertising is to communicate the promise or benefit—to convey what the brand stands for. A "reason why" can help make it believable.

- Pantene Pro-V promises healthy hair because of its "exclusive pro-vitamin formula that penetrates root to tip."
- Oil of Olay body wash ads promise superior skin care because the product has more moisturizer than even the best beauty bar.
- Clearasil ads promise that the product helps stop pimples before they pop up because the product works deep down where the pimples form.

LESSON **99** ——————————————

Wrap it up with a tag line.

A good tag line can sum up the ad and reinforce the brand's strategic positioning.

- "For hair so healthy it shines."
- "Pamper the skin they're in."
- "Dawn takes grease out of your way."

- "Bounty is the quicker picker upper."
- "If it's got to be clean, it's got to be Tide."
- "Get kissably close. Get Scope."
- "Choosy Moms choose Jif."
- "Cascade. So clean it's virtually spotless."

Here's another tag line:

- *Winning with the P&G 99* can make *you* a winner.

Good luck!

EPILOGUE
LIFE AFTER P&G

For most people who join P&G, it is their first job out of college and their first experience in the business world. The brand manager who decides to leave P&G for a new world of opportunities is often not prepared for just how different P&G is from the rest of the business world. My own experience is not that much different from what other former P&G brand people have described to me.

I joined P&G in 1962, worked my way up to brand manager, then decided to leave after a total of five years at the company. I didn't know for sure if it was the right decision. I liked what I was doing. But I wanted to live and work in New York, and the recruiters painted an exciting picture of a career working with a broad range of consumer-product companies. I went to work for Ogilvy & Mather—an advertising agency that had a reputation for professionalism in advertising that seemed to parallel the professionalism in marketing at P&G. I was confident that it was a good match.

Toward the end of the first week in my new position, I met with my General Foods client in White Plains, just north of New York City. Together we agreed that a new pool of commercials should be developed for the next flight of advertising, scheduled to begin in about three months.

I returned to my office and crafted a memo for the creative department that summarized the situation, detailed the objectives and strategy of the creative assignment, outlined parameters that had been discussed with the client, and detailed the next steps and a timetable. A meeting to review the rough commercial concepts that were to be developed was scheduled for the following week. I booked a conference room and sent the memo on its way.

I was in the conference room at the appointed time with my assistant account executive. No one else had come. I called the copywriter, who said he never received the memo. I went upstairs to his office, and together, we dug my memo out of a large stack of mail—none of which had been read. The power of the P&G memo didn't work—at least not with this creative person.

That was the beginning of a new lesson for me. Over the next several months, I learned that my very busy copywriter was easily distracted, overworked, and not well organized. Frequent phone calls were useful, but phone calls with an occasional office visit got even better results, especially around 10:30 A.M., his usual arrival time—with a cup of coffee, light cream.

I didn't stop writing memos. Some people in my agency responded to them and, in fact, complimented me on how well I wrote. That was unfortunate. Because that encouraged me to continue to write memos that did not need to be written. Although well-written memos were important to my General Foods client, it took a while longer for me to realize that for most people in the agency the telephone or meetings were the primary means of communication. It was a useful post-P&G lesson: any form of communication is only as good as the quality of the message received.

Other former Procter & Gamble people have had similar experiences. Some have missed the in-depth support of the market research, media, or promotion departments. Others have had to adjust to new cultures—cultures that are driven by retail or financial-planning considerations, that are more risk-oriented, or that are driven more by the vision or whim of the person in charge than by the culture of the organization itself. They adjusted and moved on with their careers.

However, all the former P&G people whom I interviewed for this book feel well anchored in their P&G experience. Even those who are happy to have "escaped" the P&G environment are grateful for their experience. Two recurring themes emerged from my discussions with them. One was that the strategic approach and the thinking processes that they learned at P&G are really what is important. These cut through everything else. The other was the value of the ethical standards and the respect for others that is embedded in the P&G culture.

Most of these former employees seem to have carried the values and applied the lessons they learned at P&G to their new careers. Some were able to articulate how they applied them. Others were not so sure exactly how they applied them. As one former Procter & Gamble person put it, "We're all a product of our own experience. Obviously, P&G was a high-intensity experience, and a valuable experience in so many ways. I'm sure a lot of what I think and do is based on what I learned at Procter and I don't even know it. I don't think the Procter way is the only way, and I don't agree with everything that they think and do. But I agree with a lot of it. It's part of me."

NOTES

Introduction

P&G spends . . . more than any other company in the world, from *Advertising Age International* November 1997.

Historical information, from *Eyes on Tomorrow*.

Lesson #3

In China, for example, P&G shampoo brands . . . , from *Asian Wall Street Journal* 9/18/95.

Pampers development and marketing history, from *Research Technology Management*, July–August 1990.

Lesson #6

The history of Doc Smelser and the development of research methodologies, from *Eyes on Tomorrow*.

P&G experience with Citrus Hill, from interviews with former P&G employees.

"When a question exists . . ." Brad Butler quote, from *Eyes on Tomorrow*.

Lesson #8

"People think . . ." John Pepper quote, from P&G's "National Medal of Technology" booklet.

Statement about P&G patents and scientists, from P&G's "National Medal of Technology" booklet and *Fortune* 10/14/96.

Lesson #11

"You move ahead . . ." Neil McElroy quote, from *It Floats*.

Lesson #14

"We trapped ourselves . . ." Ed Artzt quote, from *Fortune* 3/7/94.

Lesson #18

The former P&G personnel manager's perspective of the promote-from-within policy, from Harvard Business School Case #388–114.

Lesson #20

The development of Tide and resulting capital investment, from *It Floats*.

P&G's delisting from the New York Stock Exchange, from *Eyes on Tomorrow*.

Lesson #21

"There is no . . ." Owen Butler quote, from Harvard Business School Case #9–584–047.

"A principle isn't a principle . . ." Bob Goldstein quote, from a former P&G executive.

Rely withdrawal incident, from *Eyes on Tomorrow*.

P&G compensation to DMB&B, from *The House That Ivory Built*.

Lesson #23

"It's mastery of the fundamentals . . ." Ed Artzt quote, from an address to the Wharton School, 3/2/88; transcript from Procter & Gamble.

Lesson #26

"An opinion isn't . . ." Richard Deupree quote, from *It Floats*.

"The prevailing attitude . . ." Brad Butler quote, from *Eyes on Tomorrow*.

Lesson #28

The floating Ivory soap incident, from *Eyes on Tomorrow*.

Lesson #30

"Sophisticated competition . . ." Ed Harness quote, from *Eyes on Tomorrow*.

"You don't do things . . ." Vince Lombardi quote, per Jerry Kramer, from *New York Times*, Op Ed, 1/24/97.

Lesson #32

Teel story, from *Eyes on Tomorrow*.

Lesson #36

"That acceptable third . . ." James Michener quote, from Michener's *Writer's Handbook* (NY: Random House, 1992).

Lesson #40

"taking communion" quote, from Harvard Business School Case #9–388–114.

Chapter 3 introduction and Lesson #41

Ed Harness quotes, from *Eyes on Tomorrow*.

The phosphate incident in the 1960s, from *Eyes on Tomorrow* and interviews with former P&G employees.

Lesson #42

Historical information, from *Eyes on Tomorrow*.

Lesson #47

Information on ConAgra from *New York Times* 10/30/97.

Lesson #48

"We often toss . . ." Ed Artzt quote, from Harvard Business School Case #9–388–114.

Lesson #49

Information regarding the Corporate New Ventures group, from Procter & Gamble and Harvard Business School Case #N9–897–088.

Lesson #50

"You've got to envision . . ." Ed Artzt quote, from *Fortune* 3/7/94.

"It's what you learn . . ." John Wooden quote, from *Wooden: A Lifetime of Observations and Reflections On and Off the Court*, by Coach John Wooden, with Steve Jamison. Published by Contemporary Books, Lincolnwood, Illinois, 1997.

Information relating to the retail environment, from Procter & Gamble sources, *Fortune* 3/7/94, *Business Week* 10/10/94, *Business Week* 9/9/96, and *Sales and Marketing Management* November 1996.

Lesson #51

"If it doesn't work right . . ." Ed Artzt quote, from *Fortune* 11/6/89.

Information regarding Artzt's accession and reign, from Procter & Gamble sources and *Fortune* 11/6/89 and 10/14/96, *Business Week* 10/10/94, and *Advertising Age* 3/20/95.

Lesson #53

Information on Ariel and management structures in Europe, from Harvard Business School Case #384–139.

Lesson #54

"Compete with them . . ." Ed Artzt quote, from Harvard Business School Case #391–005.

Information about P&G's experience in Japan, from Procter & Gamble sources and Harvard Business School Case #391–005.

Lesson #57

Information about multinational training, from Procter & Gamble resources and P&G case study in *Global Training*, by Sylvia B. Odenwald; Homewood, IL: Richard D. Irwin, Inc., 1993; issued by American Society for Training and Development.

Lesson #59

"Where there's no . . ." Robert Wehling quote, from *Advertising Age International* January 1998.

Lesson #60

Information about the marketing of Joy in Japan, from the *Wall Street Journal* 12/10/97.

Lesson #62

Information about Peru, from Harvard Business School Case #596–010.

Lesson #65

Information about P&G retail distribution in China, from *Asian Wall Street Journal* 9/18/95.

Lesson #83

"This kind of organization . . ." Brad Butler quote, from *Eyes on Tomorrow*.

BIBLIOGRAPHY

The editors of *Advertising Age*. *The House That Ivory Built*. Lincoln-wood, IL: NTC Business Books, 1988.

Collins, James C., and Jerry I. Porras. *Built to Last*. New York: Harper Business, a division of Harper-Collins, 1994, 1997.

Kotter, John P., and James L. Heskett. *Corporate Culture and Performance*. New York: Free Press, Maxwell Macmillan International, 1992.

Lief, Alfred. *It Floats*. New York: Rinehart & Co., Inc., 1958.

Peters, Thomas J., and Robert H. Waterman, Jr. *In Search of Excellence*. New York: Warner Books by arrangement with Harper & Row, 1982, 1984.

Shisgall, Oscar. *Eyes on Tomorrow*. New York: J. G. Ferguson Publishing, Chicago, a division of Doubleday, 1981.

Waterman, Robert H., Jr. *What America Does Right*. New York: Plume, a division of Penguin Books, 1994.

ACKNOWLEDGMENTS

Thank you John Blaney, Bert Decker, Craig Decker, Tom Wilkinson, and Dan Greenberg for your encouragement and suggestions, especially during the early stages of this book. Without you it wouldn't have happened.

Thank you Judy Stewart, Steve Marks, Dave Berger, and Marie Tully for your comments and suggestions after laboring through various iterations of the manuscript.

Thank you Holly Aikin, Ruth Artzt, Lisa Baird, Cheryl Bachelder, Chris Bachelder, Don Baker, Theresa Bannon, Frank Baynham, Juelene Beck, Richard Beckhard, Tim Benton, Nat Bickford, Jack Calhoun, Roger Cameron, Gibby Carey, Jim Collins, Bill Cordes, Neil DeFeo, Steve Dennis, Kathleen Dillon-Carroll, Mike Dooley, Eric Evans, Tom Faxon, Hope Felton-Miller, John Ferries, Jim Ferguson, Pat Fettig, Jane Fox, Julie Fox, Rich George, Tom Greenbaum, David Grocer, Susan Haas, Diane Harris, Brad Hoffman, Matt Jarvis, Paul Kadin, Isaac Kavalan, Russ Klein, Ellen Lady, Fred Lamparter, Cathy Risk Linder, Jim Lisher, Joe Mack, Bob McMath, Bruce Miller, Bill Phillips, Gene Plummez, Steve Price, Andrea Rassin-Brady, Jim Schadt, Rick Snyder, Gary Stibel, Steve Stoller, Walter Solomon, Jay Stockwell, Ken Vargha, Tom Weigman, Roger Winter, and Rich Wong for your perspectives and anecdotes.

Thank you Charlotte Otto, Wendy Jacques, and Ed Rider at Procter & Gamble for your cooperation and for the information you provided.

Thank you Katharine for transcribing some of the interviews and listening to what must have seemed like intermi-
nable conversations that Mom and I had about the book.

Most of all, thank you Carol for your uninhibited criticism
of four versions of the manuscript, for your unwavering
support as the project moved forward in all its fits and
starts, for the gourmet dinners you had waiting for me after
a long day on the telephone or word processor and, above
all, for just being with me at the end of the day.

ABOUT THE AUTHOR

CHARLES L. DECKER manages a consulting and focus-group research business. After graduating from Dartmouth College and serving in the U.S. Coast Guard, he joined Procter & Gamble and was promoted to brand manager in less than three years. P&G's marketing and management principles and practices served him equally well at Ogilvy & Mather, where, as management supervisor of the Kimberly-Clark account, he and his team achieved extraordinary success for the Huggies disposable diapers brand, a direct competitor of P&G's Pampers and Luvs. He was also executive vice president at Bates Worldwide and director of their Latin American network of agencies.